Obeying God rather than man

Biblical prisoners of conscience

Obeying God rather than man

Biblical prisoners of conscience

Geoff Henstock

The Christadelphian

404 Shaftmoor Lane, Hall Green, Birmingham B28 8SZ, UK

2016

First published 2016

© 2016 The Christadelphian Magazine and Publishing Association

ISBN 978 0 85189 342 6 (print edition)
ISBN 978 0 85189 343 3 (electronic edition)

Printed and bound in Malta by
Gutenberg Press Limited

Contents

Foreword

OBEYING God is a crucial commitment of every disciple of Christ where there is a conflict with the laws, customs or commonly held views of whatever human society in which we find ourselves resident. It is an essential part of loving God "with all our hearts", which is the first and greatest commandment.

This has always been the case – sin is by definition ignoring, defying or contradicting the commandments of our Heavenly Father and the Lord Jesus Christ. There is a continual conflict between the ways of the world and the ways of God which can never be fully resolved until the return of the Lord Jesus Christ. In the meantime, would-be disciples have to face many challenges to their consciences – challenges which the scriptures tell us will become more and more difficult in the last days.

How can we cope with these challenges?

The best answer is by prayer and careful reading of God's word, which is why this book uses the examples of the trials faced by servants of God in the past to draw valuable lessons for disciples in the present. These things "were written down for our instruction, upon whom the end of the ages has come", writes the Apostle Paul to the ecclesia at Corinth. Those men and women we read about in the Bible may have lived in other ages and societies, but were just like us in facing these challenges. How they responded will therefore help us in the challenges we face, so that we too may learn to cope with whatever difficulties our lives may bring and come at last to that joyful time when God's glory will fill the earth and righteousness prevail.

John Botten
Solihull
March 2016

Introduction

G ENESIS is a book of beginnings, and the record of the Garden of Eden is the beginning of the beginning. In Genesis 3 there are familiar words which carry a wide breadth of meaning. For our purposes in this book we are interested in their message about a perpetual enmity. Genesis 3 records man's fall and the consequent judgement on Adam and Eve. In verse 15, judgement also is pronounced against the serpent:

> "I will put enmity between thee and the woman, and between thy seed and her seed; it shall bruise thy head, and thou shalt bruise his heel." (Genesis 3:15)

There is a natural and perpetual enmity between the seed of the woman and the seed of the serpent. In other words, there is perpetual enmity between the spirit and the flesh. We know from our own bitter experience that this is so at a personal level; it is true also in relation to every manifestation of the spirit and the flesh. In the institutional or corporate sense, therefore, we should expect that there will be enmity between the world and all its institutions and the ecclesia. It is inevitable that at least tension, and very often open antagonism, should mark the relationship between the world and the ecclesia. Even when foolishly we try, it simply is not possible to maintain successfully a life that is both in the ecclesia and in the world. As James says:

> "Know ye not that the friendship of the world is enmity with God? whosoever therefore will be a friend of the world is the enemy of God." (James 4:4)

In the modern world, and in particular in the western world, we live in societies that are amazingly tolerant of Christadelphians. Even though we stand apart from the society in which we live, often openly rejecting its attitudes, for the most part we are dealt with courteously. We must not, however, be lulled into thinking that toleration of us by the authorities means we are fully accepted. There is always an underlying tension – "enmity", to use the term of Genesis 3 – in our relationship with the authorities. At present it surfaces in the context of voting, which in Australia and a small number of other nations is compulsory, military service, jury duty and similar issues. In some countries it can also become an issue in at least some areas of government employment. For the most part today, then, the tension is real but it is not difficult to manage.

Making a stand
Enmity between the state and the ecclesia becomes much more obvious and problematic when there is conscription for military service. This forces brothers and sisters in Christ to make a stand against the authorities, one that is not always treated with the tolerance we encounter from the government and our neighbours when, for instance, we refuse to vote. If the country in which we are pilgrims actually is at war when it tries to conscript us, the response of the authorities might be even more aggressive and unpleasant than it is when conscription is in place during peacetime, but even then, generally speaking (at least in the English-speaking world), the brotherhood has been richly blessed because the authorities have been generous towards us as conscientious objectors. What hardships they have imposed in the form of directing brethren to undertake work of national importance were entirely reasonable when compared to the hardships faced by their neighbours who entered military service.

Of course in some parts of the world our brethren are not so blessed. Under the former regime in South Africa, for instance, our brethren who refused military service routinely were imprisoned for several years during which some suffered isolation and abuse. But their plight was infinitely better than that faced by brethren today in some non-English-speaking countries where there is no provision for exemption from military service. In at least one case during World War Two, a young brother in Germany was executed for refusing military service.

In this book we shall look at examples from scripture of brethren who made a stand for the things of God and who suffered imprisonment and loss of liberty for their stand. God was with them in their suffering. As Brother John Carter wrote:

"The narratives in the Bible of the lives of men of God in past times illustrate how God's power was exercised on their behalf in the unseen Ways of Providence. His hand is not shortened. The record was written for our instruction, that through the comfort of these scriptures we might have hope. In the attitude expressed in the words 'commit the keeping of their souls in welldoing' we provide the required basis for the exercise of divine power on our behalf."[1]

The example of these faithful saints of old is a powerful exhortation to us as we continue to stand up for the Truth in the face of the relatively benign enmity which most of us experience in these days. Should conditions deteriorate in the future or we find ourselves living under less tolerant regimes, we may become subject to aggressive and direct opposition from the authorities. In this case, their example will strengthen our resolve to endure.

---

1   J. Carter, *The Letter to the Ephesians*, The Christadelphian Magazine and Publishing Association, 1944, page 88.

Joseph

GOD'S hand is clearly evident in the life of Joseph and he was conscious of that fact. He specifically told his brethren that those things he had suffered had been directed by God with the purpose of ensuring the family's deliverance:

> "Joseph said unto his brethren, Come near to me, I pray you. And they came near. And he said, I am Joseph your brother, whom ye sold into Egypt. Now therefore be not grieved, nor angry with yourselves, that ye sold me hither: for *God did send me* before you to preserve life. For these two years hath the famine been in the land: and yet there are five years, in the which there shall neither be earing nor harvest. And *God sent me* before you to preserve you a posterity in the earth, and to save your lives by a great deliverance. So now *it was not you that sent me hither, but God*: and he hath made me a father to Pharaoh, and lord of all his house, and a ruler throughout all the land of Egypt." (Genesis 45:4-8)

The divine purpose

This is a key point. At this time Joseph had been elevated to great power and honour in Egypt, but before that he had endured considerable suffering at the hands, firstly, of his brothers and then of the Egyptians. His sufferings were not evidence, however, of God's displeasure with Joseph or of God's disregard for his welfare. On the contrary, they were part of a divine scheme by which God would redeem His people. Three times, in verses 5, 7 and 8, Joseph specifically says that it was God who sent him to Egypt. As he says in verse 7, he endured these things "to save the lives of his brethren by a great deliverance". We can appreciate, of course, how in these dramatic terms Joseph becomes a type of the Lord Jesus Christ who endured great contradiction of sinners and considerable suffering for the deliverance of his brethren.

There is an important message for us in this passage. Sometimes we might find ourselves suffering adverse consequences because of our stand for the Truth. For some brethren this has involved imprisonment or even death. For most of us, however, it will take a much less severe form – alienation from family, exclusion or ridicule from work mates, perhaps the loss of a job. Whatever form suffering takes, it is not evidence that God has forsaken us or that He disapproves of us. On the contrary, it might well be evidence that in His care for us He is moulding our character, developing our spiritual perception and even perhaps delivering us from evil.

His brothers' animosity
Joseph suffered the loss of liberty twice during his pilgrimage. On the first occasion in Genesis 37 it was at the hands of his brethren. They were spiritually less developed than Joseph and unreasonably jealous of his divinely ordained place in God's plan. Already annoyed that he was treated with special favour by their father, Joseph further aggravated his brothers by brashly speaking to them of dreams God had revealed to him that spoke of his future elevation. Sometime later, when opportunity presented itself, they conspired to eliminate him. In Genesis 37 Jacob sent Joseph to see how his brothers were getting on while away from home with the flocks. This was their chance:

> "When they saw him afar off, even before he came near unto them, they conspired against him to slay him. And they said one to another, Behold, this dreamer cometh. Come now therefore, and let us slay him, and cast him into some pit, and we will say, Some evil beast hath devoured him: and we shall see what will become of his dreams." (Genesis 37:18-20)

The majority of them wanted to kill their brother. These verses throb with the animosity and antipathy they felt towards Joseph. Reuben intervened and convinced them not to kill him. He proposed what verse 22 says was a ruse by suggesting that they leave to him to die of thirst in a pit:

> "Reuben said unto them, Shed no blood, but cast him into this pit that is in the wilderness, and lay no hand upon him; that he might rid him out of their hands, to deliver him to his father again."

Of course Reuben intended to deliver him from the pit. The word for pit (Hebrew, *bowr*) describes a pit hole, especially one used as a cistern or prison. Empty cisterns sometimes were used as prisons. The word occurs several times in Psalms in a figurative sense referring to the grave, the ultimate prison from which escape in human terms is impossible (e.g., Psalm 28:1; 30:3; 88:4; 143:7).

The brothers agreed to Reuben's suggestion and imprisoned their brother in a nearby pit:

> "It came to pass, when Joseph was come unto his brethren, that they stript Joseph out of his coat, his coat of many colours that was on him; and they took him, and cast him into a pit: and the pit was empty, there was no water in it."
>
> (Genesis 37:23,24)

A waterless pit

Consider the expressive language of verse 24. It was not just a pit, it was an *empty* pit and there was *no water* in it. There was no hope of escape because there was nothing Joseph could use to extricate himself. And there was no water to sustain him. As they were away with the flocks it is likely that this was summer, and in Canaan at that time of year a man would not last long out in the open without water.

In Zechariah 9 there is another pit without water. The prophet speaks of deliverance for prisoners incarcerated in a waterless pit. The words are exactly the same as those used in Genesis. Verse 9 demonstrates that this is a messianic prophecy:

"Rejoice greatly, O daughter of Zion; shout, O daughter of
Jerusalem: behold, thy King cometh unto thee: he is just, and
having salvation; lowly, and riding upon an ass, and upon
a colt the foal of an ass. And I will cut off the chariot from
Ephraim, and the horse from Jerusalem, and the battle bow
shall be cut off: and he shall speak peace unto the heathen:
and his dominion shall be from sea even to sea, and from the
river even to the ends of the earth. As for thee also, by the
blood of thy covenant I have sent forth thy prisoners out of
the pit wherein is no water."   (Zechariah 9:9-11)

The intervention of God through His Son was required
to effect deliverance for these prisoners in a waterless pit. They
could not deliver themselves – only the blood of the covenant
could effect their deliverance. We can see from this passage that
there is a sense in which Joseph represents all of us who are by
nature imprisoned in a waterless pit. But thanks be to God that,
through the blood of the covenant, we can be delivered from that
wretched state, for it could be effected in no other way.

Joseph's brothers, except for Reuben, intended him to die,
but they sought to avoid the act of killing him by placing him
in a waterless pit. Psalm 69 is a messianic psalm describing the
awful sufferings of our Lord. Its terms, however, are appropriate
to Joseph, albeit they speak of a man facing death by drowning
rather than death by thirst. That small detail aside, the sentiments
in Psalm 69 are remarkably apposite to the case of Joseph:

"Save me, O God; for the waters are come in unto my soul. I
sink in deep mire, where there is no standing: I am come into
deep waters, where the floods overflow me. I am weary of my
crying: my throat is dried: mine eyes fail while I wait for my
God. They that hate me without a cause are more than the
hairs of mine head: they that would destroy me, being mine
enemies wrongfully, are mighty: then I restored that which I
took not away."   (Psalm 69:1-4)

Like our Lord, Joseph was hated without valid cause. He
may have been insensitive in the way he presented the facts about
his role, but he spoke only what was true. Those who sought to

oppose him were placing themselves in opposition to the divine will. And the enemies who responded so viciously were his own flesh and blood:

"I am become a stranger unto my brethren, and an alien unto my mother's children. For the zeal of thine house hath eaten me up; and the reproaches of them that reproached thee are fallen upon me." (verses 8,9)

Ignorant of Reuben's plan, Joseph would have thought that there was no man to save, so he looked to the arm of God to bring salvation, just as the Psalmist did:

"But as for me, my prayer is unto thee, O LORD, in an acceptable time: O God, in the multitude of thy mercy hear me, in the truth of thy salvation. Deliver me out of the mire, and let me not sink: let me be delivered from them that hate me, and out of the deep waters. Let not the waterflood overflow me, neither let the deep swallow me up, and let not the pit shut her mouth upon me. Hear me, O LORD; for thy lovingkindness is good: turn unto me according to the multitude of thy tender mercies. And hide not thy face from thy servant; for I am in trouble: hear me speedily. Draw nigh unto my soul, and redeem it: deliver me because of mine enemies. Thou hast known my reproach, and my shame, and my dishonour: mine adversaries are all before thee. Reproach hath broken my heart; and I am full of heaviness: and I looked for some to take pity, but there was none; and for comforters, but I found none." (verses 13-20)

These words apply most directly to the Messiah, of course, but they have application to all saints who might suffer at the hands of evil men. Just as God was there for His Son, so He was there for Joseph. He answered Joseph's prayer and delivered him from the pit, albeit not in the way Joseph might have wanted or Reuben had planned.

Psalm 88 is another psalm that describes the plight in which Joseph found himself. It likewise has messianic overtones, but the language has striking parallels to the case of Joseph:

"O LORD God of my salvation, I have cried day and night before thee: let my prayer come before thee: incline thine ear unto my cry; for my soul is full of troubles: and my life draweth nigh unto the grave. I am counted with them that go down into the *pit*: I am as a man that hath no strength: free among the dead, like the slain that lie in the grave, whom thou rememberest no more: and they are cut off from thy hand. Thou hast laid me in the lowest *pit*, in darkness, in the deeps."   (Psalm 88:1-6)

The word "pit" in verses 4 and 6 is the same word used in Genesis 37 of the pit into which Joseph was cast. In Psalm 88:8 the Psalmist notes that his enemies were acquaintances of his, in Joseph's case his own brothers. In verse 15 the Psalmist laments that this had been his experience since his youth. In the RSV the meaning is a little clearer: "afflicted and close to death from my youth up."

Sold into slavery
This was the sad experience of Joseph – the victim of his own brothers. The record tells us that the brothers added avarice to the catalogue of their sins. They decided to sell their brother into slavery rather than leave him to die in the pit. The callousness of most of his brothers comes out in the casual terms we read in Genesis 37:

"They sat down to eat bread: and they lifted up their eyes and looked, and, behold, a company of Ishmeelites came from Gilead with their camels bearing spicery and balm and myrrh, going to carry it down to Egypt. And Judah said unto his brethren, What profit is it if we slay our brother, and conceal his blood? Come, and let us sell him to the Ishmeelites, and let not our hand be upon him; for he is our brother and our flesh. And his brethren were content."   (verses 25-27)

These were men brought up in the ecclesia of the living God. They were instructed in the ways of God; they knew about the covenant God had made with their forefathers. And yet their conscience had been seared to this degree that they could eat a relaxed meal and then discuss an opportunity to make some money by selling their own brother.

We cannot be certain, but the way the text reads in verse 25 suggests they may have had this meal quite close to the pit. Were they able to hear their brother's desperate pleas for deliverance? If so, it would be further evidence of their hard-heartedness. It is a solemn warning to recognise how easily the "old man" can assert himself even in those who have been exposed to the Truth. In a sense, the Truth in the hearts and minds of Joseph's brothers was a prisoner, captive to the baser elements of their nature. Let us resolve always to allow the Truth full liberty in our conscience.

In verse 28 they extracted Joseph from the pit, no doubt raising his hopes, only to dash them by selling him to a passing Midianite trading caravan on its way to Egypt. It seems they suspected that Reuben intended to deliver Joseph because they kept him in the dark about this transaction.

So Joseph again suffers the loss of his liberty and is taken to Egypt where he is sold as a slave. Slavery can be a wretched existence. It is a morally enervating practice in any society. When life is cheap and slaves are plentiful there is little incentive to make their lives pleasant or even bearable. Many of the slaves at the market the day Joseph was sold would have endured thoroughly miserable conditions.

Joseph, however, was fortunate. He was purchased by a high-ranking official, Potiphar, described as "an officer of Pharaoh" (Genesis 37:36; 39:1). Although the Hebrew word can mean any trusted officer its primary meaning is 'a eunuch'.[1] It was common practice in ancient times to castrate key officers who occupied positions of trust, especially if such men had access to the royal household. Hence Daniel and his friends in exile in Babylon were entrusted to "the prince of the eunuchs" (Daniel 1:7).

---

1   The word is translated eunuch in the Septuagint, Young's Literal Translation and the New English Bible.

Genesis 39:1 also specifically says that Potiphar was "an Egyptian". It might appear to be superfluous to describe a high-ranking official in Egypt as an Egyptian, so we must presume that the fact is significant. It is believed that at the time of Joseph Egypt was ruled by a foreign family; there is every reason to believe that these rulers of foreign descent would prefer to surround themselves with indigenous officials who could not pose a threat by producing offspring, especially through relationships with the royal family. We cannot be absolutely certain whether Potiphar literally was a eunuch, but it seems at the very least highly likely. If so, that might explain some of the conduct of his wife and even his relatively restrained response to the allegation that Joseph had sought to seduce his wife.

Potiphar noticed Joseph's personal qualities and raised him to a position of honour in his household:

"His master saw that the LORD was with him, and that the LORD made all that he did to prosper in his hand. And Joseph found grace in his sight, and he served him: and he made him overseer over his house, and all that he had he put into his hand. And it came to pass from the time that he had made him overseer in his house, and over all that he had, that the LORD blessed the Egyptian's house for Joseph's sake; and the blessing of the LORD was upon all that he had in the house, and in the field. And he left all that he had in Joseph's hand; and he knew not ought he had, save the bread which he did eat. And Joseph was a goodly person, and well favoured."

(Genesis 39:3-6)

Let us not misunderstand this situation. Joseph still had no effective control over his own affairs and activities, but he did enjoy a position of great trust and privilege, albeit as a slave. Curiously this has also been the experience of many of our brethren who have been imprisoned for conscientious objection. There are examples where their personal integrity has been noted by the authorities and they have been granted privileges denied to others.

Put into prison

Of course being the recipient of such privileges can be a mixed blessing, because it will expose us to greater scrutiny and can place us in compromising positions. Had Joseph, for instance, remained a drawer of water and a hewer of wood it is unlikely that he ever would have had much exposure to his master's wife. As it was, his elevated position in the household exposed him to Potiphar's wife on a regular basis, who became besotted by Joseph. As a faithful Hebrew he resisted the temptation, but this only seemed to make him more attractive to her. The fury of the woman scorned then replaced her lust and she fabricated a story about alleged infidelity. Once again Joseph became an innocent victim of incarceration because of his commitment to the ways of God:

> "Joseph's master took him, and put him into the prison, a place where the king's prisoners were bound: and he was there in the prison."   (Genesis 39:20)

It may not be obvious, but there was a degree of mercy in this punishment. As well as being called "an officer of Pharaoh", he is described as "captain of the guard" (Genesis 37:36; 39:1). The KJV margin renders this more correctly as "chief of the slaughtermen, or executioners". A man in this position would have been able to impose a capital sentence, but he spared Joseph's life and imprisoned him rather than executing him. His leniency may be a reflection of Potiphar's personal circumstances or due to previous such behaviour on the part of his wife. Perhaps it also is evidence of the high regard in which he held Joseph. Whatever the reason, Joseph's personal integrity is likely to have been a contributing factor.

This word for prison[2] in verse 20 differs from the word used earlier for "pit", although in Genesis 40:15 and 41:14 it speaks of Joseph being thrown into a dungeon. In those places the Hebrew word is exactly the same as the one used for the pit in Genesis 37.

---

2   Hebrew *cohar*, a dungeon or castle, a fortified place having walls.

This Egyptian prison or dungeon would have been a most unpleasant environment – it is likely to have been vermin-ridden and putrid – and Joseph would have been surrounded by the dregs of Egyptian society, in addition to men like himself who simply had fallen foul of their superiors. There would be few comforts and even less compassion. We may be certain that many men who entered such dungeons in Egypt disappeared without trace.

Psalm 105 rehearses some of the history of God's dealings with Israel to remind them of how He worked through providence to effect the deliverance of the nation. In Psalm 105 there is a little detail provided about Joseph's experiences in the Egyptian prison, a detail not included in the Genesis record:

"He sent a man before them, even Joseph, who was sold for a servant: whose feet they hurt with fetters: he was laid in iron: until the time that his word came: the word of the LORD tried him. The king sent and loosed him; even the ruler of the people, and let him go free." (Psalm 105:17-20)

This again says that God was directing the events of Joseph's life to deliver Israel. Verse 18 tells us a little about the rigorous punishment Joseph endured in prison. The RV translates the second half of verse 18 as, "he was laid in chains of iron".

"The LORD was with Joseph"

Here is presented the Truth in chains. Not for any wrongdoing, indeed on the contrary, he was imprisoned and shackled because he refused to do wrong. Verse 19 says that God tried Joseph for a period. He was to be delivered in the end, but not immediately. The example of Joseph confirms a vital fact: no matter how desperate our plight might appear in human terms, no matter how deep the pit in which we find ourselves, no matter how dank, dark and vicious the dungeon into which we are cast, the saints of God are never beyond the reach and care of God.

In Genesis 39 the next verses in the record reiterate what we read in Psalm 105. Even in this vile place God blessed Joseph:

"But the LORD was with Joseph, and shewed kindness unto him, and gave him favour in the sight of the keeper of the prison. And the keeper of the prison committed to Joseph's hand all the prisoners that were in the prison; and whatsoever they did there, he was the doer of it. The keeper of the prison looked not to any thing that was under his hand, because the LORD was with him; and that which he did, the LORD made it to prosper." (Genesis 39:21-23, RV)

As Psalm 105 implies, although verse 21 appears to flow straight on from verse 20, there is no reason to think that Joseph experienced this blessing immediately. He would have committed his situation to God in prayer and would have had to wait for the deliverance he sought. It might have been a considerable period before God responded in the way described. In due course, however, Joseph was elevated again to a position of honour, but still a prisoner denied personal liberty. The life of even an honoured prisoner would have been quite unpleasant, even if it did mean the end of fetters and shackles. We have a hint of that in chapter 40 when Joseph interprets the dreams of the butler and the baker. When Joseph told the butler he was to be released from prison and restored to his former position he implored him to remember him:

"Have me in thy remembrance when it shall be well with thee, and shew kindness, I pray thee, unto me, and make mention of me unto Pharaoh, and bring me out of this house."
(Genesis 40:14, RV)

Joseph wanted to be delivered from the prison. There was nothing wrong with that. We are called upon to endure the challenges that come our way as God seeks to discipline us, but there is nothing wrong with seeking an appropriate means of escape from difficulties when that is possible and consistent with the ways of truth. Martyrdom might be our lot, but it need not be sought unnecessarily. There is no virtue in enduring suffering that can be avoided without the compromise of our faith.

Joseph's plea to the butler was echoed about two thousand years later by another man who was enduring punishment, albeit in that case the punishment was just. The echo is more obvious in the ESV:

> "Only *remember me*, when it is well with you, and please do me the kindness to mention me to Pharaoh, and so get me out of this house."   (Genesis 40:14, ESV)

'Remember me and act mercifully towards me when you are elevated.' This earnest plea of Joseph was likewise the request of the penitent thief being crucified along with the Lord Jesus Christ.

> "And he said, 'Jesus, remember me when you come into your kingdom.'"   (Luke 23:42, ESV)

This is a rare case recorded in the Gospels of a man addressing the Lord as Jesus (see also Mark 1:24; Luke 4:34). In spite of the fact that he recognises Jesus' imminent ennoblement he does not address him in a formal hierarchical sense as master or lord; he uses his personal name. The language used by the thief suggests both intimacy and confidence – an intimacy and a confidence that may be shared by the Lord's brethren who, like this repentant thief, are "crucified with Christ" (Galatians 2:20).

Delivered from prison

Unlike our Lord who never forsakes those who put their trust in him, in Genesis 40:23 the ungrateful butler forgot Joseph's kindness; and in Genesis 41:1 we learn that Joseph had to endure another two years in prison. Again, God intervened to ensure Joseph's deliverance. He caused Pharaoh to dream a dream that troubled him. The conscience-smitten butler remembered Joseph's ability to interpret dreams and suggested that Pharaoh seek advice from Joseph. The response of Joseph in verse 16 is very instructive:

> "Then Pharaoh sent and called Joseph, and they brought him hastily out of the dungeon: and he shaved himself, and changed his raiment, and came in unto Pharaoh. And Pharaoh said unto Joseph, I have dreamed a dream, and there is none that can interpret it: and I have heard say of thee, that when thou hearest a dream thou canst interpret it. And Joseph

answered Pharaoh, saying, It is not in me: God shall give Pharaoh an answer of peace."   (Genesis 41:14-16, RV)

Joseph's response to Pharaoh is a model for all saints. There was no petulant pouting about the injustice of his imprisonment, nor any vain claim to special powers or gifts. Joseph firmly but respectfully acknowledged that God held the answer and that he was merely God's servant. In a much lesser sense we are similarly gifted in relation to the things of the future. Our understanding of prophecy gives us insights into the future of the nations, but any honour that accrues from that insight rightly belongs to God.

Joseph became a better man through the things that he suffered. As a young man he had been a little forward in his approach. He lacked sensitivity when speaking about the privileged position to which God clearly was calling him. It was not that what he said was wrong – it was entirely correct. The problem was that he did not take account of the impact of the way he presented it to his brothers and even his parents.

There is a lesson in this for us. We have been called to a position of great privilege and honour. God has called us out of the nations to become one with Him and with His Son. In addition, through the word of God we have been granted insights into His plan and purpose with this earth. It is right that we should witness to the wonder of God's grace and seek to warn our neighbours of the judgement to come upon this earth. But when we do, let us reflect the sober, measured and mature style of Joseph in Genesis 41 and not the brash approach of the immature Joseph we met earlier in chapter 37.

Joseph was required to undergo severe trials involving alienation from his family, the loss of liberty and even binding in fetters and chains. All this was part of God's scheme to effect the deliverance of His people. In this regard Joseph is, of course, a type of Christ. He is also a great encouragement to us. We know that it is through much tribulation that we shall enter the kingdom of God. Our Lord said it is inevitable that trial must come. We must not regard suffering and trial, even imprisonment, as evidence that we have been forsaken or that we are out of favour with God. On the contrary, these difficult circumstances may be designed to develop us spiritually. No matter how severe and prolonged they might be, we may be sure that they will not overwhelm us if we retain our faith in God. The concluding words of Romans 8 are very apt in this respect:

"Who shall lay anything to the charge of God's elect? It is God that justifieth; who is he that shall condemn? It is Christ Jesus that died, yea rather, that was raised from the dead, who is at the right hand of God, who also maketh intercession for us. Who shall separate us from the love of Christ? shall tribulation, or anguish, or persecution, or famine, or nakedness, or peril, or sword? Even as it is written, For thy sake we are killed all the day long; we were accounted as sheep for the slaughter. Nay, in all these things we are more than conquerors through him that loved us. For I am persuaded, that neither death, nor life, nor angels, nor principalities, nor things present, nor things to come, nor powers, nor height, nor depth, nor any other creature, shall be able to separate us from the love of God, which is in Christ Jesus our Lord."

(Romans 8:33-39, RV)

Jeremiah

J EREMIAH is a man to whom we ought to be able to relate because he was a faithful Israelite living at the end of an age. Judgement was looming – in fact during his lifetime Judah felt the impact of that judgement in many ways. The society in which he lived was corrupt and decadent, although it retained some nominal awareness of the Almighty. The world in which he lived was being destabilised by competing powers seeking to dominate the Middle East. In many ways the situation in which Jeremiah ministered was one that is very similar to our own today.

A promise of deliverance

Jeremiah faced a formidable task in proclaiming God's will and the certainty of impending judgement to a corrupt society that really did not wish to hear. It is clear from chapter one that God appreciated how difficult was the task before Jeremiah. At the commencement of his ministry God reassured Jeremiah that He would deliver him from his adversaries:

"The LORD said unto me, Say not, I am a child: for to whomsoever I shall send thee thou shalt go, and whatsoever I shall command thee thou shalt speak. Be not afraid because of them: for I am with thee to deliver thee, saith the LORD. Then the LORD put forth his hand, and touched my mouth; and the LORD said unto me, Behold, I have put my words in thy mouth: see, I have this day set thee over the nations and over the kingdoms, to pluck up and to break down, and to destroy and to overthrow; to build, and to plant."

(Jeremiah 1:7-10, RV)

These are extraordinary words. When did Jeremiah personally fulfil the words of verse 10? He was unable to effect significant moral change in his own land during his lifetime, and he certainly never exercised authority over the nations. But the message he presented dealt with the pulling down of fleshly strongholds; it prophesied the destruction of the kingdom of men and spoke eloquently of the planting of God's kingdom in Israel.

In verse 8 God promised Jeremiah that He would deliver him. Few men have received such an unambiguous and direct promise. Few of God's servants were in such need of just that reassurance. The opposition Jeremiah faced was extreme. Ruthless men who felt threatened by his resolute ministry were determined to silence his message, and they were prepared to put him to death if that was the only way it could be achieved. In this, his circumstances mirror those that confronted our Lord.

A similar message today

As extraordinary as this promise is to Jeremiah, it is no more astonishing than the promise of God to us. Like Jeremiah we have been commissioned to preach the Gospel of the coming kingdom and to warn all who would listen of impending judgement. Our message is remarkably similar.

Jeremiah's basic message is given a geographic focus in verses 14,15:

"And the word of the LORD came unto me the second time, saying, What seest thou? And I said, I see a seething caldron; and the face thereof is from the north. Then the LORD said unto me, Out of the north evil shall break forth upon all the inhabitants of the land. For, lo, I will call all the families of the kingdoms of the north, saith the LORD; and they shall come, and they shall set every one his throne at the entering of the gates of Jerusalem, and against all the walls thereof round about, and against all the cities of Judah."

(Jeremiah 1:13-15)

In our day we likewise often seek to warn our neighbours of a judgement that will sweep down upon Israel from the north. It will come upon a modern Israel at least as worldly and corrupt as the Judah described in verse 16. And it is a judgement of direct personal relevance to the people to whom we preach. Implicit in our preaching, as in the case of Jeremiah, is a forthright denunciation of the corrupt and evil nature of the society in which we live.

Our obligation to preach is very similar to that imposed upon Jeremiah. Only a few of us, however, will face the kind of opposition that confronted him. Most of us will meet nothing more threatening than a lack of interest. But if like Jeremiah we are required to face strong opposition from the state or from the society around us, we may be confident that God will deliver us as He delivered Jeremiah in his day. In fact, God has already delivered us through the blood of His Son. No matter what the world might do to us our deliverance is sure.

Aggressive opposition

At the end of chapter one God reiterates His promise to stand by Jeremiah in all his trials:

> "Thou therefore gird up thy loins, and arise, and speak unto them all that I command thee: be not dismayed at them, lest I dismay thee before them. For, behold, I have made thee this day a defenced city, and an iron pillar, and brasen walls, against the whole land, against the kings of Judah, against the princes thereof, against the priests thereof, and against the people of the land. And they shall fight against thee; but they shall not prevail against thee: for I am with thee, saith the LORD, to deliver thee."   (Jeremiah 1:17-19, RV)

The prophet once again is encouraged not to allow the vicious opposition he would face to distract him from his mission. Verse 19 makes it clear that, in spite of God's promise, he would still encounter aggressive opposition. Hence we can appreciate why this repeated message was necessary to buttress him against the challenges ahead.

The repeating of this encouragement does not indicate that God thought Jeremiah would not believe Him. In an earlier age Joshua had likewise been encouraged repeatedly to "be strong and of a good courage" (Joshua 1:6,7,9,18). In each case the repetition of the exhortation is a reflection not of the weakness of the individual concerned but of the magnitude of the challenges they were to face in the discharge of their mission as a servant of God. Let us draw strength from the repeated encouragement of all the servants of God who were called upon to make a stand for the Gospel.

Sometimes Jeremiah is presented as stern, taciturn and humourless, blithely proclaiming bleak messages of doom and gloom. That certainly is the 'popular press' view of the man, so much so that his name has become an epithet for a negative person who always has a message of despair and hopelessness. His name has also spawned the word 'jeremiad' to describe doleful lament. That perception of Jeremiah is entirely unfair. Not only are there many very glorious and uplifting messages sprinkled through the book, and even in Lamentations, but Jeremiah himself was in fact a wondrously warm and sensitive person. He certainly was very passionate.

The chronology of the book of Jeremiah is notoriously complex and uncertain. Chapter 26, however, is unambiguously dated. We know from verse 1 that the events described are at the very start of Jehoiakim's reign. At that time Jeremiah's uncompromising messages incurred the intense wrath of all the leaders in Judah; verse 8 specifically mentions the religious rulers as well as the secular rulers. Jeremiah condemned the nation and its leaders for their evil ways. The leaders' initial inclination was to kill him:

> "It came to pass, when Jeremiah had made an end of speaking all that the LORD had commanded him to speak unto all the people, that the priests and the prophets and all the people laid hold on him, saying, Thou shalt surely die. Why hast

thou prophesied in the name of the LORD, saying, This house shall be like Shiloh, and this city shall be desolate, without inhabitant? And all the people were gathered unto Jeremiah in the house of the LORD."   (Jeremiah 26:8,9, RV)

Verses 20-23 record the case of another prophet, Urijah, who pronounced exactly the same words as Jeremiah and who was slain by the hand of the king personally. His case demonstrated that these men were willing to murder anyone to whom they were opposed. Jeremiah was under very real threat, but God had promised that he would be delivered. So it is that at the end of chapter 26 Ahikam is raised up to provide the deliverance promised in chapter one:

"But the hand of Ahikam the son of Shaphan was with Jeremiah, that they should not give him into the hand of the people to put him to death."   (Jeremiah 26:24, RV)

An emotional roller-coaster

If we go back a few chapters we come to the events recorded in chapter 20, which most students believe occurred during the reign of Jehoiakim. Here we find that Jeremiah's bold stand in the face of such a vicious and hostile society took a heavy toll on his sensitive nature. That is clear from the words of the prophet:

"O LORD, thou hast deceived me, and I was deceived: thou art stronger than I, and hast prevailed: I am become a laughing-stock all the day, every one mocketh me. For as often as I speak, I cry out; I cry, Violence and spoil: because the word of the LORD is made a reproach unto me, and a derision, all the day. And if I say, I will not make mention of him, nor speak any more in his name, then there is in mine heart as it were a burning fire shut up in my bones, and I am weary with forbearing, and I cannot contain. For I have heard the defaming of many, terror on every side. Denounce, and we will denounce him, say all my familiar friends, they that watch for my halting; peradventure he will be enticed, and we shall prevail against him, and we shall take our revenge on him."
     (Jeremiah 20:7-10, RV)

These are words of anguish and pain. In verse 9 he admitted he was tempted to abandon his ministry, but the spirit of God within him made it impossible for him to hold back. As with our Lord Jesus Christ, the road he was required to tread might have been unavoidable, but that fact did not make it any easier. In verse 11 he recalled the promises of God from chapter one:

"But the LORD is with me as a mighty one and a terrible: therefore my persecutors shall stumble, and they shall not prevail: they shall be greatly ashamed, because they have not dealt wisely, even with an everlasting dishonour which shall never be forgotten."   (Jeremiah 20:11)

Yet, having brought this to mind, in the remaining verses of chapter 20 he bemoaned the fact that he was even born if he had to endure such hardship. Jeremiah was on an emotional roller-coaster as he considered his lot.

Insensitive men might be tempted to ask why Jeremiah should have been so distressed in view of what God had promised so clearly, and of the evidence of God's power to deliver Jeremiah so recently demonstrated in the person of Ahikam. If we are tempted to think this way, we should make allowance for what Jeremiah had just been forced to endure, for it appears to have been that experience which triggered these words.

Put in the stocks
In chapter 19 the prophet had delivered an enacted parable about the coming judgement on Jerusalem. The leaders, including the king in verse 3, witnessed the message but they were completely unmoved. Actually, strictly speaking that is not true. At least one of them was moved to action, but not repentance. In chapter 20 Pashur, a leading official in the temple, turned on Jeremiah:

"Now Pashhur the son of Immer the priest, who was chief officer in the house of the LORD, heard Jeremiah prophesying these things. Then Pashhur smote Jeremiah the prophet, and put him in the stocks that were in the upper gate of Benjamin, which was in the house of the LORD."   (Jeremiah 20:1,2, RV)

In verse 6 we learn that Pashur was a false prophet. No doubt he had felt slighted by Jeremiah's stern rebuke of the false prophets. Now he could exact revenge. He flogged Jeremiah and then placed him in the stocks. The Hebrew for "stocks" is *mahpeketh*. Literally it means twisting or distortion (see Gesenius). It seems that the contraption used was designed in a way that ensured the body was not just restrained but deliberately distorted in an agonising fashion for maximum discomfort. The word is used only four times in the Bible. Three of those occasions relate to Jeremiah (see 20:2,3; 29:26). The only other reference to stocks is found in 2 Chronicles 16:10, where there is a clear parallel with Jeremiah's case.

Just like Pashur in Jeremiah 20, in 2 Chronicles 16 King Asa turned against another prophet who uttered a message of judgement that he did not want to hear. Hanani the seer had come to Asa and condemned him for aligning Judah with Syria:

"At that time Hanani the seer came to Asa king of Judah, and said unto him, Because thou hast relied on the king of Syria, and hast not relied on the LORD thy God, therefore is the host of the king of Syria escaped out of thine hand."

(2 Chronicles 16:7, RV)

In verses 8 and 9 Hanani elaborated on what was in store for Judah, just as Jeremiah would do on so many occasions at a later stage, and the king responded in raging fury:

"Then Asa was wroth with the seer, and put him in the prison house; for he was in a rage with him because of this thing. And Asa oppressed some of the people the same time."

(verse 10, RV)

The RSV says Asa "put him in the stocks, in prison". It is the same punishment Jeremiah would be forced to endure. This treatment meted out to the prophets of the Lord is a salutary lesson for all generations. Let us never despise the word of God, no matter how confronting it might be. Faithful men such as Hanani, Isaiah and Jeremiah paid a heavy price that the word of God might be proclaimed.

In Hanani's case, 2 Chronicles 16:10 specifically tells us that the stocks were located within the prison. That was not always the case. In Jeremiah 20 we find that Pashur, no doubt with one eye on his own advancement, placed Jeremiah in the stocks in a particular spot. These stocks were not located in the prison but near the "high gate of Benjamin". It could be that Pashur wanted to maximise Jeremiah's shame by placing him on exhibition in a public place, but there may be even more to it than this. Jeremiah 38 tells us something significant about the gate of Benjamin:

"Now when Ebed-melech the Ethiopian, one of the eunuchs which was in the king's house, heard that they had put Jeremiah in the dungeon; the king then sitting in the gate of Benjamin ..."   (Jeremiah 38:7)

At that time the king sat at the gate of Benjamin to dispense justice. It was a very public place. Vast numbers of the people of Jerusalem would see Jeremiah being punished in a place normally associated with the dispensing of justice. His incarceration there would have been seen as a royal rebuke. The king disliked Jeremiah at least as much as Pashur and would have been able to gloat over his predicament.

An uncompromising message

The world is like this at times – vindictive and cruel. It delights sometimes in humiliation. For some, merely coming out on top is not enough. There will be times when we have to endure public shame for the sake of the Gospel, although admittedly not usually as extreme as that suffered by Jeremiah. In modern times, some brethren who refused to do military service during times of war received white feathers in the mail; a white feather was a recognised symbol of cowardice. Some even were confronted personally by people who gave them a white feather in the street. Jeremiah's steadfastness ought to encourage us to endure whatever the world throws at us.

As painful as it must have been for Jeremiah, his limbs confined and twisted, he was able to condemn the wicked Pashur in strong and uncompromising terms:

"Then said Jeremiah unto him, The LORD hath not called thy name Pashur, but Magor-missabib. For thus saith the LORD, Behold, I will make thee a terror to thyself, and to all thy friends: and they shall fall by the sword of their enemies, and thine eyes shall behold it: and I will give all Judah into the hand of the king of Babylon, and he shall carry them captive into Babylon, and shall slay them with the sword. Moreover I will deliver all the strength of this city, and all the labours thereof, and all the precious things thereof, and all the treasures of the kings of Judah will I give into the hand of their enemies, which shall spoil them, and take them, and carry them to Babylon. And thou, Pashur, and all that dwell in thine house shall go into captivity: and thou shalt come to Babylon, and there thou shalt die, and shalt be buried there, thou, and all thy friends, to whom thou hast prophesied lies."

(Jeremiah 20:3-6)

Jeremiah's suffering did not blunt his message. When we take into account the context we can see that the tone of despair in Jeremiah's pleas in the rest of the chapter was certainly not the petty whingeing of a weak and timid soul.

"I am shut up"

Time marched on, and in Jeremiah 36 the prophet had another run-in with Jehoiakim. He had not been cowed by his previous humiliation. It was now the fourth year of Jehoiakim's reign and the prophet appears to be subject to some kind of detention. In verse 5 of chapter 36 we read Jeremiah's instructions to Baruch:

"Jeremiah commanded Baruch, saying, I am shut up; I cannot go into the house of the LORD: therefore go thou, and read in the roll, which thou hast written from my mouth, the words of the LORD in the ears of the people in the LORD's house upon the fasting day: and also thou shalt read them in the ears of all Judah that come out of their cities."

(Jeremiah 36:5,6)

The term "shut up" is the Hebrew word *atsar*, meaning literally 'enclosed'. It is translated "restricted" by the NASB. In

chapter 33:1 and 39:15 the same word is used to describe the
prophet's detention in prison.[1] The word is also used of David
when he was confined in Ziklag seeking refuge from Saul, another
corrupt king (1 Chronicles 12:1).

On this occasion the word appears to indicate that
Jeremiah was under house arrest or at least a ban from attending
the temple. Some have suggested that Jeremiah might have been
subject to some form of ceremonial uncleanness that prohibited
him from attending the temple. We cannot be dogmatic about
the impediments to which he was subjected at this time, but we
may be certain that he was not actually in prison because in verse
19 his supporters suggested that he flee to a secret hiding place.

The imperishable word of God

Although "shut up" or confined, the prophet has access to Baruch
and he gave him a message to read in the temple. There were
still some faithful leaders in Judah and they recognised these
words as a powerful message from Almighty God. They wanted
to present this message before the king, but knew there was a
risk that he would react violently, so they took steps to protect
the prophet and Baruch:

> "Then said the princes unto Baruch, Go, hide thee, thou and
> Jeremiah; and let no man know where ye be. And they went
> in to the king into the court, but they laid up the roll in the
> chamber of Elishama the scribe, and told all the words in the
> ears of the king."   (Jeremiah 36:19,20)

The king heard the message and commanded that the
scroll be brought to him. In a pathetic gesture he tried to destroy
the words of which he did not approve. The words had an impact
on the decadent rulers, but not in the right way. This is a case of
the Truth in the form of the Gospel message being enchained.
The king tried to destroy the word of God! It is hard to believe
that an occupant of the throne of David could behave in such a

---

1   This is also the Hebrew word used in Jeremiah 20:9 when Jeremiah says the word
    of God "was in mine heart as a burning fire *shut up* in my bones".

way. But the word is imperishable, and in verse 32 the scroll that
had been destroyed was replaced.

We are reminded, perhaps, of those tragically misguided
church leaders in the Middle Ages and even later who sought
to suppress the Truth by burning Bibles that had been printed
to enlighten the masses. We might think of book burning as a

Bishop Tunstall of London burning Tyndale's translation of the New Testament.

hallmark of totalitarian dictatorships like those of Stalin or the Nazis, but the Roman Catholic system was hundreds of years ahead of those tyrannical regimes.

In 1380 John Wycliffe completed his translation of the Bible into English. He wrote a preface which included these words which certainly would prove to be true of his own fate and which might well have been inspired by the example of Jeremiah:

"God grant us to ken and to keep Holy Writ, and to suffer some paine for it at the last."

The Roman Catholic authorities in England persecuted those who supported Wycliffe and who had the audacity to read God's word. Some of those executed for possessing a copy of the Bible were burnt at the stake with copies of the translation tied around their neck. The example of Jeremiah and of others who have been persecuted for daring to stand fast to the word of God should make us reflect on our own attitude towards God's word. Do we who live in tolerant societies cherish it more than life and liberty itself? Or do we allow the tolerance of our age to diminish our commitment to the revealed will of God?

The Papal system was never going to succeed in suppressing God's word, and neither would Jehoiakim. Men might ignore the clear signs of the times and the evidence of impending judgement, but that judgement will come regardless. Let us not make the mistake of ignoring or turning our back on passages of the Bible whose message we find distasteful or inconvenient.

Again in verse 26 God intervened to protect Jeremiah. He was not in prison at this time, but the prophet's liberty had been taken away. He could not go out and about safely:

"The king commanded Jerahmeel the son of Hammelech, and Seraiah the son of Azriel, and Shelemiah the son of Abdeel, to take Baruch the scribe and Jeremiah the prophet: but the LORD hid them."   (Jeremiah 36:26)

Detained in prison

Later, in the reign of Zedekiah, as the nation sank further and further, things got even harder for Jeremiah. In chapter 32 he was detained in prison, apparently because his prophecies that Judah would fall to Babylon were seen as evidence of sympathy with the enemy:

"The word that came to Jeremiah from the LORD in the tenth year of Zedekiah king of Judah, which was the eighteenth year of Nebuchadrezzar.[2] For then the king of Babylon's army besieged Jerusalem: and Jeremiah the prophet was shut up in the court of the prison, which was in the king of Judah's house. For Zedekiah king of Judah had shut him up, saying, Wherefore dost thou prophesy, and say, Thus saith the LORD, Behold, I will give this city into the hand of the king of Babylon, and he shall take it; and Zedekiah king of Judah shall not escape out of the hand of the Chaldeans, but shall surely be delivered into the hand of the king of Babylon, and shall speak with him mouth to mouth, and his eyes shall behold his eyes; and he shall lead Zedekiah to Babylon, and there shall he be until I visit him, saith the LORD: though ye fight with the Chaldeans, ye shall not prosper?"   (Jeremiah 32:1-5)

Here is an important lesson for us. While we must be circumspect about how we present the Gospel, especially prophecies about the future and coming judgements, we also must be forthright and clear in our message. There are times when the world will not want to hear that message, but that does not absolve us from our duty to preach. Jeremiah was not being provocative when he spoke about the conquest of Judah by Babylon. He merely spoke the truth. But as the nation came under more and more stress, whatever tolerance he had enjoyed began to evaporate. The same is true for us. In times of peace and prosperity the state often will be very tolerant, but when the nation or society is under threat tolerance often diminishes.

His trials intensify

In chapter 37, at the start of Zedekiah's reign, Jeremiah was a free man. He was someone for whom the king had some respect:

---

2   The eighteenth year of Nebuchadnezzar is of significance in terms of the events described in Daniel 3.

"Zedekiah the king sent Jehucal the son of Shelemiah and Zephaniah the son of Maaseiah the priest to the prophet Jeremiah, saying, Pray now unto the LORD our God for us. Now Jeremiah came in and went out among the people: for they had not put him into prison."   (Jeremiah 37:3,4)

Here is that unusual phenomenon that may be experienced even by modern believers in Western society. A truly decadent, immoral leader has a measure of respect for the word of God. Perhaps in this case, and in the case of leaders today, it is a residue of the culture that they have inherited from their forefathers. Whatever the reason for such men having some respect for the word of God it is unable to be translated into a meaningful and humble response, a submissive response to God's declared will and purpose. Curiosity and respect for the literary value of the Bible are no alternatives for repentance.

In verses 6 to 10 Jeremiah uttered a prophecy about the impending fall of Jerusalem, and for this he incurred the wrath of the ruling classes. They accused him of being a Babylonian sympathiser, and in verses 14 to 16 they imprisoned him:

"Then said Jeremiah, It is false; I fall not away to the Chaldeans. But he hearkened not to him: so Irijah took Jeremiah, and brought him to the princes. Wherefore the princes were wroth with Jeremiah, and smote him, and put him in prison in the house of Jonathan the scribe: for they had made that the prison. When Jeremiah was entered into the dungeon, and into the cabins, and Jeremiah had remained there many days."

These men were particularly vicious, and the prison into which they placed Jeremiah would not have been a pleasant place. In verse 16 it is described as a dungeon. This is the same Hebrew word that was used of the prison in which Joseph was incarcerated. Did Jeremiah derive some strength from this link with Joseph and the knowledge that God had delivered Joseph from his trials? Jeremiah was imprisoned, verse 16 says, for an extended period, so he might well have had opportunity to ponder the fate of faithful servants in earlier days.

Zedekiah, a vacillating, weak man, appears to have had something of a soft spot for Jeremiah. In verse 17 he (eventually) delivered the prophet from the prison and asked him if he has any message from God:

"Then Zedekiah the king sent, and took him out: and the king asked him secretly in his house, and said, Is there any word from the LORD? And Jeremiah said, There is: for, said he, thou shalt be delivered into the hand of the king of Babylon. Moreover Jeremiah said unto king Zedekiah, What have I offended against thee, or against thy servants, or against this people, that ye have put me in prison? Where are now your prophets which prophesied unto you, saying, The king of Babylon shall not come against you, nor against this land?"
(verses 17-19)

Jeremiah had an opportunity to relieve his suffering but he refused to compromise. The message he had from God might not be popular with the king but that was what he would be told regardless. Here is another lesson for us: we must never be tempted to trim the word of God or seek to minimise the harsh realities for personal gain. By all means we should present a balanced and positive picture of God's plan and purpose, but we must never censor those elements that might trouble our friends and neighbours just so we can avoid unhappy consequences.

The next verse is very significant:

"Therefore hear now, I pray thee, O my lord the king: let my supplication, I pray thee, be accepted before thee; that thou cause me not to return to the house of Jonathan the scribe, lest I die there."   (verse 20)

Jeremiah pulled no punches, but that did not mean he had no interest in his own well-being. The conditions in that dungeon must have been appalling. Clearly Jeremiah thought he was likely to die if he remained there. He implored the king to show him some mercy in spite of the fearsome message he delivered. The king responded and eased the conditions for Jeremiah:

"Then Zedekiah the king commanded that they should commit Jeremiah into the court of the prison, and that they should

give him daily a piece of bread out of the bakers' street, until
all the bread in the city were spent. Thus Jeremiah remained
in the court of the prison."   (verse 21)

"Let this man be put to death"

The prophet was not released from detention, but his conditions
were eased considerably. The reference to Zedekiah making
provision for food is interesting. In ancient Israel, as in many
countries, men who fell foul of the authorities would be either
executed or imprisoned. Those in prison ordinarily would be
provided with food. But the fact that Zedekiah made a specific
commandment in this case seems to suggest that the princes
that had imprisoned Jeremiah had not provided him with food,
or at least sufficient food. They wanted him to die. Many of them
would have been among the rulers under Jehoiakim who, in
chapter 26, wanted Jeremiah to die. I think this helps to explain
the tone of anxiety in Jeremiah's plaintive plea to be delivered
from the prison.

The king's generous gesture incurred the wrath of his more
vicious underlings. In chapter 38 they again turned on Jeremiah
when he continued to preach about the coming judgement. It is
interesting to note the names of those who opposed Jeremiah:

"Then Shephatiah the son of Mattan, and Gedaliah the son of
Pashur, and Jucal the son of Shelemiah, and Pashur the son
of Malchiah, heard the words that Jeremiah had spoken unto
all the people ..."   (Jeremiah 38:1)

The name "Pashur" occurs twice in this verse. We have
already seen that a man named Pashur persecuted Jeremiah
in the days of Jehoiakim in chapter 20. We presume that this
"Pashur the son of Malchiah" is not the Pashur of chapter 20,
for that man was the son of Immer. But it is possible the man
described in this verse as "Gedaliah the son of Pashur" is the son
of the false prophet Jeremiah had condemned in chapter 20. If
so, that might account for the virulence of his attitude towards
Jeremiah. We cannot be certain of such a connection, but it is
curious that two men named Pashur might be referred to in

this context. Whatever the facts, these wicked princes conspire against Jeremiah:

> "Therefore the princes said unto the king, We beseech thee, let this man be put to death: for thus he weakeneth the hands of the men of war that remain in this city, and the hands of all the people, in speaking such words unto them: for this man seeketh not the welfare of this people, but the hurt." (verse 4)

Note their clearly stated intention. They do not wish just to imprison Jeremiah: they openly declare that he should die. This seems to have been their intention previously and the king's graciousness only made them more determined than ever. Zedekiah's response epitomises the weakness of this pathetic king:

> "Then Zedekiah the king said, Behold, he is in your hand: for the king is not he that can do any thing against you."
>
> (verse 5)

I am only the king, how can I resist you? What an indictment! Abdicating all authority, like Pilate he washed his hands and delivered an innocent man to be murdered. The wicked princes imprison Jeremiah again, this time in even more distasteful conditions than he had experienced in chapter 37:

> "Then took they Jeremiah, and cast him into the dungeon of Malchiah the son of Hammelech, that was in the court of the prison: and they let down Jeremiah with cords. And in the dungeon there was no water, but mire: so Jeremiah sunk in the mire." (38:6)

Their stated intention was to kill Jeremiah. This dungeon, which appears to have been a disused and silted up cistern, would have been unsanitary and vile. The mire was a thick, sticky sludge. It takes only a little imagination to picture the putrid scene described so graphically in verse 6.

Others enduring similar indignities

Other saints have endured similar vile conditions at various times. One instance is recorded by Brother Alan Eyre in *The*

Protesters,[3] which gives a graphic description of the sufferings of a group of men and women who may have shared our beliefs and who were imprisoned for their faith in Zurich, Switzerland, in 1525. There are remarkable parallels with the experience of Jeremiah. These protesters fell foul of the rulers, who were fellow Protestants, but who did not share their commitment to the word of God. In effect they were being persecuted by their own people, rather like Jeremiah who suffered more at the hands of Jews than he ever did at the hands of the Babylonians.

At their trial the famous Protestant leader Zwingli "personally and enthusiastically advocated the summary execution of all the accused". The sentence, however, was more merciful:

"... to lie in the tower on a diet of bread, water and apple sauce, with no one permitted to visit them, as long as seems good to God and my lords."

Brother Eyre then quotes a description of their fate written by Dr. Balthasar Hübmaier, one of the accused who escaped imprisonment at least initially:

"Over twenty men, widows, pregnant wives, and maidens were cast miserably into dark towers, sentenced never again to see sun or moon as long as they lived, to end their days on bread and water, and thus in the dark towers to remain together, the living and the dead, until none remained alive – there to die, to stink, and to rot. Some among them did not eat a mouthful of bread in three days, just so that others might have to eat."

These people must have found some comfort in their knowledge that saints in other ages had suffered similar indignities and that this was not evidence that God had forsaken them.

Zedekiah's weakness
It only adds to Zedekiah's shame that it takes a Gentile, an Ethiopian, to bring the king to his senses and ensure that justice

---

3   A. Eyre, *The Protesters*, The Christadelphian Magazine and Publishing Association, 1985 (Second Edition), pages 38,39.

is done for Jeremiah. In Jeremiah 38:7 it is recorded that the king went one day to his usual place for dispensing justice: in verse 9 Ebed-melech presented the case for Jeremiah's release. The king responded positively to the appeal, even though he had cowered before the princes earlier, and asked Ebed-melech to release Jeremiah.

After his release Zedekiah sought advice from the prophet. The king was told that his only hope lay in surrendering to the Babylonians. If he did so, he would live and the city would not be burned. Zedekiah was reluctant – or unable – to accept that advice because he feared that Jews who already had defected to Babylon would persecute him (see verses 17-19). Jeremiah responded that it was not those who had defected to Babylon who posed a threat to Zedekiah, but the princes who remained in Jerusalem and who had so poorly advised the king. The prophet drew upon his own experience in the miry dungeon to illustrate how the king's wives would taunt Zedekiah as they went into captivity:

> "If thou refuse to go forth, this is the word that the LORD hath shewed me: And, behold, all the women that are left in the king of Judah's house shall be brought forth to the king of Babylon's princes, and those women shall say, Thy friends have set thee on, and have prevailed against thee: thy feet are sunk in the mire, and they are turned away back."
>
> (verses 21,22)

The Jerusalem Bible has the wives derisively referring to Zedekiah's advisers as "your fine friends"! Their flawed advice sealed the fate of the king and of the city. Jeremiah had sunk into literal mire and he had to be physically dragged out. Zedekiah's feet also would become stuck in the mire but there would be no Eded-melech to deliver him.

Enduring to the end

Jeremiah, having been delivered from the miry cistern, remained in custody, albeit in more comfortable circumstances, until the kingdom fell and the Babylonians triumphed. Ironically he then

secured his release from a Gentile power which might have been
expected to have no respect for the God that he served. As we
shall see, the final siege of Jerusalem coincided with the events
of Daniel 3 and the outcomes of those events may have had an
influence on the way Jeremiah was treated.

Jeremiah 39 records the fall of Jerusalem to the
Babylonians. Although the leadership under Zedekiah was
treated harshly, Nebuzar-adan, described in the KJV as "captain
of the guard", was charged with looking after Jeremiah:

"Now Nebuchadrezzar king of Babylon gave charge concerning
Jeremiah to Nebuzar-adan the captain of the guard, saying,
Take him, and look well to him, and do him no harm; but do
unto him even as he shall say unto thee." (Jeremiah 39:11,12)

Nebuzar-adan's title is better rendered as "chief of the
executioners" (Young) or "chief of the royal executioners"
(Rotherham; see also the KJV margin for verse 9). The word
translated executioner, meaning 'slayer', is used of only three
personages in the Old Testament – Nebuzar-adan in both 2 Kings
25 and Jeremiah, a cook (in the sense of one who slaughters and
prepares an animal for food) in 1 Samuel 9, and of Potiphar in
Genesis 37:36, 39:1, etc. It is curious to note this further link
between the records of Joseph and Jeremiah, albeit Joseph
suffered at the hand of the chief executioner, whereas Jeremiah
was blessed by a man with the same position.

There is another contrast between Jeremiah's 'blessing' at
the hand of Nebuzar-adan and the case of Joseph. Jeremiah 40
opens with the prophet in chains (verse 1), presumably chains
with which his countrymen had bound him prior to the fall of
Jerusalem. The chief executioner loosed him from those chains
(verse 4), and gave him a choice as to his future. Joseph also is
said to have been subjected to fetters of iron (Psalm 105:18),
although the words used are different from those used in relation
to Jeremiah. Whether Joseph was put in chains by Potiphar
cannot be determined with certainty, but what is certain is that
the Egyptian chief executioner did not extend any mercy to his
captive once he had imprisoned him.

Jeremiah endured to the end. We may be sure, therefore, that like Paul there is a crown laid up for him. Jeremiah's example of steadfast devotion to the service of his God and his uncompromising commitment to preaching the Gospel should inspire us to meet whatever challenges the world presents.

Daniel and his friends

W HAT impressive young men were Daniel and his three friends! Almost certainly only teenagers at the beginning of the book, the first we learn about them in chapter one proves that by every criterion regarded as important by man they were fine young men:

"The king spake unto Ashpenaz the master of his eunuchs, that he should bring certain of the children of Israel, and of the king's seed, and of the princes; children in whom was no blemish, but well favoured, and skilful in all wisdom, and cunning in knowledge, and understanding science, and such as had ability in them to stand in the king's palace, and whom they might teach the learning and the tongue of the Chaldeans." (Daniel 1:3,4)

Temptation

Daniel and his friends represented the cream of the crop, the flower of their generation: young, good looking, highly intelligent, well educated and cultured. In every natural sense they were fine young men, and they were given the opportunity to share in the best that Babylon could offer:

"And the king appointed them a daily provision of the king's meat, and of the wine which he drank: so nourishing them three years, that at the end thereof they might stand before the king." (verse 5)

What a temptation this must have been for Daniel and his friends – young men, far away from home, with little hope of

Judah being restored in their lifetime. Now in the centre of world
power and influence they are being offered an express lane to
the best the world could offer. Most young men would have been
sorely tempted. Pride could easily have lifted them up, as they
became aware of the possibilities opening to them. They could be
forgiven for thinking that perhaps they would be able to use their
privileges to advantage their people. Many young brothers over
the years have succumbed to the lure of much lesser opportunities.

In addition to this material temptation, in Daniel 1:7
these four young Israelites who had names which referred to the
graciousness and overshadowing care of the God of Israel were
given new names which commemorated the idols of Babylonian
religion or belittled the God of Israel:

- Daniel ('God is my judge') was called Belteshazzar ('Beltis[1] defend the king');
- Hananiah ('Yah is gracious') was called Shadrach ('I am fearful [of God?]');
- Mishael ('Who is as God?') was called Meshach ('I am of little account');
- Azariah ('God is helper') was called Abed-nego ('Servant of Nebo').

It would seem that these young men were among those
Israelites taken to Babylon as hostages by Nebuchadnezzar,
probably during the campaign described in 2 Kings 24. There are
difficulties with the chronology of this period[2] and it is impossible
to be certain when Daniel, Hananiah, Mishael and Azariah came
to Babylon, but it is clear that they arrived as young men and, at
least in Daniel's case, remained there in exile until very aged. The
table opposite is a suggested chronology for the book of Daniel.

It would have been daunting for these faithful young
Israelites to find themselves in exile in Babylon. Henry Milman
eloquently describes how confronting it must have been:

---

1 Beltis is a form of the title of the wife of Marduk or Bel, the patron deity of
   Babylon.
2 Brother Edmund Green discusses the chronological difficulties associated with the
   arrival of Daniel in Babylon in *The Prophecy of Daniel*, pages 15,16.

Passage	Year BC	Indicator	Event	Daniel's age
Daniel 1:1	606	Third year of Jehoiakim	Daniel taken into exile?	14
Daniel 2:1	603	Second year of Nebuchadnezzar	Nebuchadnezzar's dream	17
Daniel 3:1 (LXX)	587	Eighteenth year of Nebuchadnezzar	Nebuchadnezzar's image	33
Daniel 4	573-569		Nebuchadnezzar's humiliation	47-51
Daniel 7:1	553	First year of Belshazzar	Vision of the four beasts	67
Daniel 8:1	551	Third year of Belshazzar	Vision of ram and he goat	69
Daniel 5	539	Last year of Belshazzar	Writing on the wall	81
Daniel 5:31	539	Darius the Mede takes over	Fall of Babylon	81
Daniel 6	539		Daniel in the lions' den (Daniel 6)	81
Daniel 9:1	539	First year of Darius the Mede	Daniel intercedes for Israel and Seventy Weeks prophecy	81
Daniel 1:21	536	First year of Cyrus of Persia	Decree to rebuild Jerusalem (Ezra 1:1)	84
Daniel 10-12	534	Third year of Cyrus of Persia	Daniel's last prophecy	86

"Nothing could present a more striking contrast to their native country than the region into which the Hebrews were transplanted. Instead of their irregular and picturesque mountain city, crowning its unequal heights, and looking down into its deep and precipitous ravines, through one of which a scanty stream wound along, they entered the vast, square, and level city of Babylon, occupying both sides of the broad Euphrates, while all around spread immense plains, which were intersected by long straight canals, bordered by rows of willows. How unlike their national temple – a small but highly furnished and richly adorned fabric, standing in the midst of its courts on the brow of a lofty precipice – the colossal temple of the Chaldean Bel, rising from the plain, with its eight stupendous stories or towers, one above the other, to the perpendicular height of a furlong! The palace of the Babylonian kings was more than twice the size of their whole city: it covered eight miles, with its hanging gardens built on arched terraces, each rising above the other, and rich in all the luxuriance of artificial cultivation. How different from the sunny cliffs of their own land, where the olive and the vine grew spontaneously, and the cool, shady, and secluded valleys, where they could always find shelter from the heat of the burning noon."[3]

Conscientious objectors

Many teenagers away from home and alone in such an alluring city would succumb to temptation, and who could blame them? Fortunately these young Hebrews were not alone. In addition to all the natural qualities Daniel 1:4 describes, these men possessed another and more important attribute, one that would not have been obvious to the Babylonians. Even at such a young age they were men of strong and determined faith who knew the God of Israel was with them:

3 Henry Hart Milman, *The History of the Jews*, Volume 1, page 323 (Everyman's Library edition).

"But Daniel purposed in his heart that he would not defile himself with the portion of the king's meat, nor with the wine which he drank: therefore he requested of the prince of the eunuchs that he might not defile himself ... Then said Daniel to Melzar, whom the prince of the eunuchs had set over Daniel, Hananiah, Mishael, and Azariah, Prove thy servants, I beseech thee, ten days; and let them give us pulse to eat, and water to drink. Then let our countenances be looked upon before thee, and the countenance of the children that eat of the portion of the king's meat: and as thou seest, deal with thy servants."   (Daniel 1:8,11-13)

In verses 11 and 12 it appears that Daniel is spokesman for all four young men, imploring Melzar to respect conscience. They were *conscientious objectors*, resisting the dictates of the rulers of the nation where they lived as strangers and pilgrims because to obey would clash with their beliefs. And note the respectful tone Daniel adopts: firm, but with no hint of arrogance. This is a pattern for all saints in all ages when called upon to resist the demands of secular society. The example of these young men also reminds us that one of the great challenges of conscientious objection is that it impacts disproportionately on the young who are, for that reason, often the least experienced.

Daniel and his friends were committing their ways to God. In faith they trusted that He would care for them. We know the story. Melzar was gracious towards them and the young men thrived on the simple diet that ensured their faith was not compromised by inappropriate involvement with the arrangements instituted by the king.

The king's dream
A few years later, through the providence of God, Daniel was given an opportunity to present himself before Nebuchadnezzar. The king had dreamed a dream which troubled him and none of the wise men of Babylon could relieve his anxiety by interpreting the dream. In his fury and frustration the king determined to slay all the wise men of Babylon (Daniel 2:12), which would have

included Daniel and his friends. Having appealed for time to understand the matter, Daniel and his companions prayed that God would reveal to them the meaning of the dream (verses 16-18).

God revealed the dream to Daniel and he told the king he could provide the interpretation that was so eagerly desired. His response to the king is very telling:

> "The king answered and said to Daniel, whose name was Belteshazzar, Art thou able to make known unto me the dream which I have seen, and the interpretation thereof? Daniel answered in the presence of the king, and said, The secret which the king hath demanded cannot the wise men, the astrologers, the magicians, the soothsayers, shew unto the king; but there is a God in heaven that revealeth secrets, and maketh known to the king Nebuchadnezzar what shall be in the latter days."   (Daniel 2:26-28)

In many respects Daniel's response to Nebuchadnezzar reflects that of Joseph's when he interpreted Pharaoh's dream. Daniel did not express outrage at the petulance of the king's decree that all the wise men be killed, nor did he seek to claim supernatural powers or to elevate himself in the eyes of the king. Like Joseph, Daniel stated that it was not he who reveals secrets about what will happen in the kingdom of men, but God.

The vision which Daniel went on to outline and interpret is a cornerstone of God's prophetic plan. Building on this vision, Bible students can develop remarkable insights into God's plan and purpose with this earth. The later prophecies in Daniel build on the record of the image revealed to Nebuchadnezzar, and the imagery in the book of Revelation in turn builds on Daniel's vision. History as it has unfolded since those days confirms the accuracy of these visions. Having seen so much history unfold exactly as these prophecies predicted we may be confident about those elements which remain to be fulfilled. Let us, however, mirror the example of Daniel by remembering that any honour relating to our insights into the future of the nations rightly belongs to God.

The message God delivered through Daniel, and no doubt his demeanour and character, impressed the king. At the end of Daniel 2 we read:

"The king answered unto Daniel, and said, Of a truth it is, that your God is a God of gods, and a Lord of kings, and a revealer of secrets, seeing thou couldest reveal this secret. Then the king made Daniel a great man, and gave him many great gifts, and made him ruler over the whole province of Babylon, and chief of the governors over all the wise men of Babylon. Then Daniel requested of the king, and he set Shadrach, Meshach, and Abed-nego, over the affairs of the province of Babylon: but Daniel sat in the gate of the king." (verses 47-49)

Daniel was elevated to a position of considerable honour and prestige and he secured the promotion of his friends. We may be sure that this was not just a case of nepotism – jobs for the boys as we might say today. From chapter 1 we know that these were highly competent young men. Daniel naturally would want around him men of great ability, especially where that ability was coupled with a strong and lively faith in God.

At this time Nebuchadnezzar was at the zenith of his power. He had been granted detailed insight into the plan and purpose of God, he was the unchallenged administrator of the best part of the civilised world and he was supported by highly competent and upright men in key government positions. This is the situation that applied as chapter 3 of Daniel unfolds.

"The king made an image"

Chapter 3 of Daniel comes after chapter 2 and before chapter 4, and the placement of the story recorded in chapter 3 is highly significant. The Bible is inspired and the order of the events recorded is part of that inspiration.

The Septuagint version of Daniel 3 commences: "In his eighteenth year[4] Nebuchadnezzar the king made an image."

---

4   Nebuchadnezzar's eighteenth year also is significant in terms of events in Judah. This was when he laid siege to Jerusalem, thus commencing the final death throes of the kingdom of Judah (Jeremiah 32:1,2).

Even though there is no textual evidence other than the Septuagint version for the reading "in his eighteenth year", many commentators think it might be correct. If so, in Daniel 3 we are sixteen years after the events described in chapter 2 (which verse 1 tells us was in the second year of the king). If this is correct, the spirit has chosen to ignore many things that must have occurred in the years in between. This is the next incident it has chosen to record. Why does this story follow immediately after Daniel 2? Brother John Thomas suggests an answer:

> "All the important characteristics of the Kingdom of Men … could not be exhibited in a compound metallic image of a man: it was, therefore, necessary to introduce other symbols for its elucidation. In the third chapter of Daniel, we are presented with an interesting illustration of the impiety and blasphemy of the Kingdom of Men; of its hostility to the people of the House of David, or the Jews … of the furnace of affliction through which they would have to pass in rejecting the superstitions of the Kingdom of Men, and in adhering to the truth of God; of their meeting with the Deliverer in their extremity; of the destruction of their tormentors; of their final deliverance; and of the ascription at last of blessing, and honour, and glory, and power to the God of Israel by the assembled nations, when God's people shall be promoted to the direction of human affairs, and the Kingdom of Men shall be no more."[5]

The great theme running through Daniel is the conflict between the Kingdom of Men and the Kingdom of God – the conflict between Babylon and Zion. It is in fact the great theme of this current mortal dispensation, as illustrated by the following chart taken from the book *The Apocalypse and History* (page 18 – see opposite). Rome in the book of Revelation is the latter-day manifestation of the Babylonian power.

---

5   J. Thomas, *Exposition of Daniel*, The Christadelphian Magazine and Publishing Association (Fourth Edition), pages 8,9.

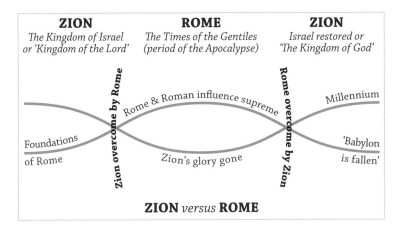

Daniel 3 exemplifies the inherent enmity between the world and the ecclesia. Verse 1 says Nebuchadnezzar set up an image of gold. Brother C. C. Walker in *Theophany* (page 123) says the image was about seventy-five feet high. Brother John Thomas in *The Book Unsealed* (page 6) suggests that it was about ninety feet high. Whatever its exact height, clearly it was huge.

The word rendered "image" is exactly the same as the word translated "image" in chapter 2. Although it could not be proven conclusively, from the manner in which the record in Daniel is constructed it seems likely that this image was modelled on the one in the vision of the previous chapter. In *Theophany* Brother C. C. Walker suggests that it was raised up by Nebuchadnezzar to commemorate the dream of Daniel 2.

The height of the image has led some to conclude that, if the idol was in the form of a man (along the lines of that seen in Nebuchadnezzar's dream) it must have been mounted on a pedestal, otherwise the proportions would have been grotesque. Brother C. A. Ladson, however, rejects this suggestion and postulates that it may have been something more sinister:

"Perhaps this was an image of one of the obscene symbols of that day, and to bow down to it would have been to sink into depths of degradation. The control exercised by the God-fearing spirit revolts at the thought even of bowing down to an image of that which is made in the image of God, even the human form; but to bow down to anything less than that would be to bow down to things that spoke only of grossness and impiety."[6]

What was true of ancient idolatrous images remains true – perhaps is even truer – of the gross and impious 'idols' to which modern men bow down in such droves. And just as the influence of the vast crowds in Babylon who worshipped this image must have been hard for the faithful Israelites to resist, so modern-day saints struggle in their efforts to stand firm against the idolatry of the age which takes the form of all those things which would compromise their commitment to the service of Almighty God.

In Nebuchadnezzar's dream only the head was made of gold. Yet in chapter 3 the whole image is gold – almost certainly gold-plated, incidentally, because a solid gold image of this size would weigh in excess of 4,000 tonnes.

In verses 2 and 3 all the senior officials are summoned to attend the dedication of the image:

"Then Nebuchadnezzar the king sent to gather together the princes, the governors, and the captains, the judges, the treasurers, the counsellors, the sheriffs, and all the rulers of the provinces, to come to the dedication of the image which Nebuchadnezzar the king had set up. Then the princes, the governors, and captains, the judges, the treasurers, the counsellors, the sheriffs, and all the rulers of the provinces, were gathered together unto the dedication of the image that Nebuchadnezzar the king had set up; and they stood before the image that Nebuchadnezzar had set up."   (Daniel 3:2,3)

Why are we twice given such a detailed list of official titles? If we were to read Daniel without reference to the chapter divisions the answer would become clear. Just a few verses prior at the end of chapter 2, we learn that Daniel and his friends were

6   C. A. Ladson, *Guided by the Star*, The Christadelphian Magazine and Publishing Association (1948), page 129.

high officials in the province of Babylon. They would, therefore, have been among those required to attend this ceremony.

"Fall down and worship"

It seems likely that they might have obeyed the command to attend the ceremony. At this stage there might have been no indication that idol worship was involved, so as law-abiding residents they would have complied, just as today a saint would comply with government requirements like a census. But in verses 4 to 6 it soon became obvious that more than attendance was required:

> "Then an herald cried aloud, To you it is commanded, O people, nations, and languages, that at what time ye hear the sound of the cornet, flute, harp, sackbut, psaltery, dulcimer, and all kinds of musick, ye fall down and worship the golden image that Nebuchadnezzar the king hath set up: and whoso falleth not down and worshippeth shall the same hour be cast into the midst of a burning fiery furnace."   (verses 4-6)

The phrase in verse 4, "O people, nations, and languages" is all-encompassing. In verse 10 it is interpreted as meaning "every man". Remember that phrase because we encounter it again.

In verse 5 we have another detailed list – this time of instruments. The playing of all these instruments together was the signal for all men to worship the image. Verse 6 says that failure to conform would bring punishment. It is ever thus. Persecution of the saints is always triggered by their refusal to conform either to the laws or the standards of the world about them.

The punishment was to be roasting in a furnace. This was a characteristic means of execution for the Babylonians. They are the only people mentioned in scripture as using such a method of execution. There is, however, another example in scripture where death was the penalty for failure to worship an image. It is particularly interesting to note that this record in Revelation 13 also is associated with fire being used to punish those who do not conform.

The image of the beast

In Daniel 3 the saints were called upon to worship an image which was the representation of the religious and political authority of the kingdom of men. Nebuchadnezzar was, of course, the religious and political leader of Babylon. All of this finds a remarkable and obviously divinely ordained parallel in Revelation 13, where there is a later manifestation of the Babylonish power:

> "And I beheld another beast coming up out of the earth; and he had two horns like a lamb, and he spake as a dragon. And he exerciseth all the power of the first beast before him, and causeth the earth and them which dwell therein to worship the first beast, whose deadly wound was healed. And he doeth great wonders, so that he maketh fire come down from heaven on the earth in the sight of men, And deceiveth them that dwell on the earth by the means of those miracles which he had power to do in the sight of the beast; saying to them that dwell on the earth, that they should make an image to the beast, which had the wound by a sword, and did live. And he had power to give life unto the image of the beast, that the image of the beast should both speak, and cause that as many as would not worship the image of the beast should be killed."
>
> (Revelation 13:11-15)

In verse 13 one of the characteristics of this system is fire coming down from heaven. In *Eureka*[7] Brother John Thomas demonstrates that this is a symbol of the persecution imposed by the political and religious forces of the Holy Roman Empire against those who would not conform and worship the beast. Thus it is an exact parallel with the record in Daniel 3.

Verse 15 speaks of worshipping the image of the beast. The Greek word for "image" here is *icon*. The same word is used in the Septuagint in Daniel 2 and 3. In Revelation 13 worship of "the image of the beast" was submission to the papal system. That papal system maintained religious and political domination and

---

7   See Volume 3, pages 321,322 (black edition).

was Babylonish in origin. It established itself in direct opposition to Almighty God and demanded the allegiance of all men. Any who opposed it were liable to be put to death. History testifies to the viciousness with which the system prosecuted its claims.

Brother John Thomas says this about the persecuting power of the image of the beast:

"Whosoever did not receive and would not submit to its oracular utterances were anathematized by it, and scathed with its fire from the heaven, or were excommunicated and penally destroyed as Heretics beyond the protection of law, the killing of whom was declared to be no murder."[8]

These also were the consequences of failing to worship the image established by 'Pope' Nebuchadnezzar.

Refusing to conform

The faithful Israelites in Babylon found themselves faced with the same fanaticism which would later confront their counterparts in the Middle Ages. The law decreed in Daniel 3:4-6 was invoked in verse 7. Evidently Daniel and his friends, despite the fact that they were known by names which linked them to the idolatry of Babylon, refused to obey, provoking this response:

"Wherefore at that time certain Chaldeans came near, and accused the Jews." (verse 8)

Perhaps these were Chaldeans who had been displaced when Daniel and his friends were elevated, or whose aspirations to power were frustrated by the presence in high office of these competent Hebrews. Whatever their motive, there is an unmistakable air of malice about these words. It is another reminder that we are always being watched, our every action scrutinised, and there are people in the world who just love to find reasons to criticise and condemn us.

Nothing infuriates the world more than our refusal to conform. These Chaldeans saw their chance to pull down these faithful men and they accused them of disobedience:

---

8   Ibid., page 328.

"There are certain Jews whom thou hast set over the affairs of the province of Babylon, Shadrach, Meshach, and Abed-nego; these men, O king, have not regarded thee: they serve not thy gods, nor worship the golden image which thou hast set up."
(verse 12)

It is curious that they choose only to indict Daniel's three friends. Was this because of the special relationship between the king and Daniel as outlined at the end of chapter 2? If so, probably they also wished to remove Daniel in the end, but decided it was better to start by cutting away his power base.

It is interesting to note that Daniel's friends may not actually have breached the law. In verse 5 there is a detailed list of instruments that were to be the signal for worship. That list is repeated exactly in verse 10 and in verse 15. Three times in eleven verses we have this detailed list word-for-word in identical form. But a careful reading of the words in verse 7, which seems to be the instance on which the Chaldeans base their charge against the Jews, reveals something significant.

Verse 5	Cornet	Flute	Harp	Sackbut	Psaltery	Dulcimer
Verse 7	Cornet	Flute	Harp	Sackbut	Psaltery	
Verse 10	Cornet	Flute	Harp	Sackbut	Psaltery	Dulcimer
Verse 15	Cornet	Flute	Harp	Sackbut	Psaltery	Dulcimer

In verses 5, 10 and 15 the instruments are listed as cornet, flute, harp, sackbut, psaltery, dulcimer and all kinds of music, but the list in verse 7 omits the dulcimer.[9] One of the instruments was missing on that occasion.

Surely it is not just a coincidence that this list differs slightly from all the others. Clearly there was a technical failure to invoke

---

9   While the dulcimer is omitted from the Hebrew text, some translations (e.g., RSV, NASB and ESV) insert the missing instrument in verse 7, following the Vulgate which inserts the omitted instrument in spite of its absence from the original Hebrew.

the law in verse 7. A legalist might point out that the precisely defined signal of verse 5 had not been given. To their credit, Daniel's friends, "the Jews" (is there a hint of anti-Semitism in the use of that epithet?), did not take that approach. Here is another lesson for us in our engagement with the world. There are times when we are tempted to shelter behind a technicality rather than take a clear and unambiguous stand for what we know to be right and proper. Let us always resolve to make a clear stand for what we believe and not exploit technicalities and loopholes in a tawdry effort to avoid making a stand.

It also is to the credit of Daniel's friends that they do not appear to have invoked Daniel's support when confronted with the accusation and when appearing before Nebuchadnezzar who verse 13 describes as enraged. In verse 15 the king gave them an ultimatum. They could obey or they could die. He finished with words he lived to regret, a boast that echoes the arrogance of Pharaoh and of Rabshakeh: "Who is that God that shall deliver you out of my hands?" Nebuchadnezzar was soon to find out the answer to that question.

In verses 16 to 18 the Jews answered the king calmly and respectfully:

"Shadrach, Meshach, and Abed-nego, answered and said to the king, O Nebuchadnezzar, we are not careful to answer thee in this matter. If it be so, our God whom we serve is able to deliver us from the burning fiery furnace, and he will deliver us out of thine hand, O king. But if not, be it known unto thee, O king, that we will not serve thy gods, nor worship the golden image which thou hast set up."

They gave Nebuchadnezzar the respect to which he was entitled but they stood firm for their conscience. Peter told the Sanhedrin that "we ought to obey God rather than men", and that was the message of the Jews to the king. Ironically their calm and respectful approach only served to enrage the king even more and he issued the command in verse 19 to make the fire seven times hotter than usual. He then ordered that they be bound and cast in.

In verse 22 it is clear that the furnace was indeed much hotter than usual, for the men who delivered the Jews into the fire perished from the extreme heat. The Jews, however, were unharmed.

Verse 21 includes a detailed list of the clothes in which Shadrach, Meshach and Abed-nego were dressed when cast into the furnace. Why do we need this detail? Daniel 3 is a chapter of detail: the officials are listed twice in verses 2 and 3 and the musical instruments are listed four times (albeit one is an incomplete list). In each case the detail adds to our appreciation of the record. So it is in the case of the clothes.

In verse 27 there is detailed commentary to emphasise just how complete was the deliverance of Daniel's friend from the fiery furnace:

> "And the satraps, the prefects, the governors, and the king's counsellors gathered together and saw that the fire had not had any power over the bodies of those men. *The hair of their heads was not singed, their cloaks were not harmed, and no smell of fire had come upon them.*" (ESV)

The miraculous nature of their deliverance is emphasised by the fact that, not only were they not killed, even their clothes were unharmed and there was even no smell of fire. The experience of Daniel's friends has reassured saints in all ages that, regardless of how hot the furnace of affliction, persecution or temptation might be, it will have no lasting impact on them if they remain faithful.

We know from the references to Daniel in the Gospels that the Jews of our Master's day were familiar with this record. The example of Daniel's friends would have been a great encouragement to our Lord and the apostles in the first century when they likewise were obliged to make a stand in the face of the virulent opposition of the rulers and the community.

Death by fire

The fate of Hananiah, Mishael and Azariah contrasts rather dramatically with that of two other Jews who Nebuchadnezzar at about the same time also condemned to death by roasting. Jeremiah records that two false prophets, Ahab and Zedekiah, were executed by Nebuchadnezzar:

> "And of them shall be taken up a curse by all the captivity of Judah which are in Babylon, saying, The LORD make thee like Zedekiah and like Ahab, whom the king of Babylon roasted in the fire; because they have committed villany in Israel, and have committed adultery with their neighbours' wives, and have spoken lying words in my name, which I have not commanded them; even I know, and am a witness, saith the LORD." (Jeremiah 29:22,23)

Did Daniel and his colleagues know of the fate of these false Jewish prophets? It certainly is possible. We do not know where Zedekiah and Ahab met their fate, but there was regular communication between Jerusalem and Babylon so the news could have reached Jews in either city. In any event, as senior officials in the government they would be aware of the effectiveness of Babylon's judicial roasting. An awareness of what happened to Zedekiah and Ahab may have made Daniel's friends apprehensive, but clearly it had no impact on their resolve to take a stand in accordance with their conscience.

Shadrach, Meshach and Abed-nego were faithful Jews and they were delivered, whereas these false prophets perished. There are occasions, however, when faithful servants may not be spared execution or suffering. In the Middle Ages some of those who made a stand and refused to worship the image system of their day also faced death by burning. And that system made "fire to come down from heaven" to punish their defiance. And lest we should comfort ourselves that this all happened centuries ago, look at the picture overleaf.

These were Protestants who were burnt to death by a Roman Catholic mob in the Italian city of Barletta in 1866! A few who are alive today can remember people who were born at about that time. It was the year when Brother John Thomas was publishing the second volume of *Eureka*. It was two years after Brother Robert Roberts commenced the magazine that later

became known as *The Christadelphian*. It was the year when the first Christadelphian was known to be baptized in Australia. If Christadelphians had been in Barletta on that day in 1866 they might have been one of these people being burnt to death!

Unlike Daniel's friends, these men and women were not delivered from death by fire. It is true that most of those who have been executed like this by the Roman Catholic system had not embraced the Truth as it is in Christ Jesus. We may be sure, however, that those of our brethren who have suffered this fate at the hands of the image system will find deliverance when our Lord returns.

A faithful witness

In verse 15 of Daniel 3 Nebuchadnezzar had arrogantly asked, "Who is that God that shall deliver you out of my hands?" He now knew.

> "Then Nebuchadnezzar spake, and said, Blessed be the God of Shadrach, Meshach, and Abed-nego, who hath sent his angel, and delivered his servants that trusted in him, and have changed the king's word, and yielded their bodies, that they might not serve nor worship any god, except their own God."
> (verse 28)

Brother C. A. Ladson sums up the significance of this record:

> "Surely here are lessons in godly self-control for every one of us, that we should guard ourselves from the spirit of vain-glory; from the spirit that would flow along with popular enthusiasm; against the rage that blinds the heart and will throw itself recklessly against God; against that envy which prompts men to the downfall of their fellows, because of jealousy, that they have been preferred to places of honour instead of them; against the hypocrisy that cloaks envy with zeal for God."[10]

The faithful witness of the saints for conscience sake can be a powerful testimony to the world about us. People notice what we do, and if we are consistent and reasonable they might respect that and in some cases will be won to the Truth. It is a somewhat controversial question, but it is possible that that is what happened in the case of Nebuchadnezzar. It is possible that the king was converted and embraced the hope of Israel. The faithfulness of Daniel and his friends may have convicted the king.

The phrase we encountered in verse 4, "O people, nations, and languages", which was used when commanding every man to worship the image, occurs again at the end of this record. Its use at the beginning and end are like bookends to the story.

---

10 C. A. Ladson, *Guided by the Star*, The Christadelphian Magazine and Publishing Association (1948), page 133.

In verse 29 we find this phrase, and again in Daniel 4:1. When Nebuchadnezzar had learnt his folly and was about to propound the doctrine that "the most high rules in the kingdom of men", he addresses his message to exactly the same group who had previously been commanded to worship the image. It is like a retraction of the error of chapter 3.

This is why it is so significant from a literary perspective that chapter 3 is recorded between chapters 2 and 4. Having toyed with trying to overturn or frustrate the will of God as revealed in Daniel 2, the king finally recognised the underlying truth revealed in his dream. In chapter 4 he penned a majestic essay on the divine oversight of earthly affairs – a fact still evident for all who have eyes to see.

Nebuchadnezzar repented of his error but his repentance had little long-term impact on Babylon. Jeremiah, a contemporary of Nebuchadnezzar, penned in chapters 50 and 51 a detailed prophecy of judgement to be unleashed upon Babylon. Within that very severe prophecy there is a poignant comment that suggests a willingness to bless Babylon, even though the willingness would be frustrated: "We would have healed Babylon, but she is not healed" (Jeremiah 51:9). Because she would not be healed, Babylon was doomed to destruction, which would be effected in the days of Nebuchadnezzar's grandson.

It is recorded in Exodus that, after Joseph died, another pharaoh arose in Egypt who knew not Joseph. Something similar happened in Daniel's day. The message Nebuchadnezzar learnt with some pain and cost in Daniel 3 was not appreciated by his descendants. The healing offered to Nebuchadnezzar was not embraced by his successors. So it was that in chapter 5 his grandson arrogantly provoked the God of Israel and was overthrown. And in chapter 6 the new ruler, Darius, had to learn the lesson of Daniel 4 for himself.

The plot against Daniel

In Daniel 3 it had been Daniel's three friends who had been tested. In chapter 6 Daniel himself is put to the test. When

Darius conquered Babylon he had to make arrangements for the administration of the empire, as recorded in Daniel 6:1,2. In verse 3 we see that the characteristics that had impressed Nebuchadnezzar when Daniel was young were evident still in his old age, and Darius appointed Daniel as his senior bureaucrat. It is thought that Daniel almost certainly was in his eighties at this time:

"It pleased Darius to set over the kingdom an hundred and twenty princes, which should be over the whole kingdom; and over these three presidents; of whom Daniel was first: that the princes might give accounts unto them, and the king should have no damage. Then this Daniel was preferred above the presidents and princes, because an excellent spirit was in him; and the king thought to set him over the whole realm."
(Daniel 6:1-3)

Darius captured Babylon in 539 BC. Imagine what the fall of Babylon meant to Daniel. A captive there for over sixty years, Daniel would have been only too well aware of Jeremiah's prophecy, uttered nearly seventy years before, about the fall of Babylon and the ending of the desolation of Judah:

"For thus saith the LORD, That after seventy years be accomplished at Babylon I will visit you, and perform my good word toward you, in causing you to return to this place."
(Jeremiah 29:10)

His yearning for Jerusalem and the land of his fathers had never left Daniel, but the fall of Babylon must have intensified his longing for the restoration of the kingdom of God. Given the circumstances Daniel was always going to be a keen observer of this new regime, looking for any hint that Darius or his successors would act to fulfil Jeremiah's prophecy. With great enthusiasm, therefore, he must have seized the opportunity to serve as Darius' Prime Minister.

As in chapter 3, jealousy motivated those who felt slighted by Daniel's elevation and they now conspired against him:

"Then the presidents and princes sought to find occasion against Daniel concerning the kingdom; but they could find none occasion nor fault; forasmuch as he was faithful, neither was there any error or fault found in him." (Daniel 6:4) The men who sought to bring down Daniel were not fools. They knew he had only one chink in his armour, and that was his unswerving faith in Almighty God and the hope of Israel:

"Then said these men, We shall not find any occasion against this Daniel, except we find it against him concerning the law of his God." (verse 5)

Having realised that his faithfulness was his Achilles heel they sought to flatter the king. Their approach is quite obsequious:

"Then these presidents and princes assembled together to the king, and said thus unto him, King Darius, live for ever. All the presidents of the kingdom, the governors, and the princes, the counsellors, and the captains, have consulted together to establish a royal statute, and to make a firm decree, that whosoever shall ask a petition of any God or man for thirty days, save of thee, O king, he shall be cast into the den of lions. Now, O king, establish the decree, and sign the writing, that it be not changed, according to the law of the Medes and Persians, which altereth not. Wherefore king Darius signed the writing and the decree." (verses 6-9)

In verse 7 they sought to inflate their position by claiming that it represented the combined wisdom of all the leaders in the empire. It is a classic technique of those in the world who oppose the saints to claim that everyone agrees with this view or is willing to act in this way. Apart from the fact that that is irrelevant, we need to be wary of such claims because often they are false. In this case the simple fact is that verse 7 is a lie. They had not consulted "all the presidents", as they claimed, because in verse 2 Daniel is the chief of these presidents.

A time of testing

Darius' pride, excited by the prospect of such honour, rose to the bait. It is likely that he did not realise the implications of the decree for his trusted servant Daniel. What does Daniel do?

This decree was of no practical benefit. He had the respect of the king and arguably from the language of verse 2 he had an implied obligation not to allow any actions that would compromise good administration in the empire. He could have reasoned, therefore, that he should plead his case before the king. He does not do this. Daniel does not use his privileged position for personal gain.

Having decided not to intervene on his own behalf, Daniel could have 'laid low'. It is only a month, he could have reasoned, and God would understand! After all, it is not like the case of his friends in chapter 3. He is not being compelled to engage in false worship, merely to refrain from the worship of the true God for only thirty days. That reasoning might have appealed to many a less committed Israelite, but not Daniel.

Daniel's response as recorded in chapter 6 is a model for all times in such circumstances:

> "Now when Daniel knew that the writing was signed, he went into his house; and his windows being open in his chamber toward Jerusalem, he kneeled upon his knees three times a day, and prayed, and gave thanks before his God, as he did aforetime." (verse 10)

Daniel acted as he had always done. He did not grandstand. He did not worship in some public place in an aggressive act of civil disobedience. He simply performed his devotions as he always did.

In World War Two the brotherhood in the English-speaking world in general was blessed in that provision was made for conscientious objection to military service. Brothers and sisters did all that they could without compromising their conscience to cooperate with the authorities and not to provoke them or the wider community. Other groups, at least in Australia, were not so cooperative. Members of the Jehovah's Witnesses community, for instance, were extremely aggressive in their relations with the government. As a consequence, the activities of the Jehovah's Witnesses in Australia were banned for the duration of the war, whereas the Christadelphians were free to continue their preaching.

When I was young I used to collect an elderly brother and take him to the meetings. He had been a Jehovah's Witness during the war and it was his job each week to mislead the police about where meetings were planned to be held. He was a type of double agent, deliberately misinforming the authorities about their activities. It is not possible to stress too strongly how inappropriate and how corrupt that kind of behaviour would be for a saint. There are no circumstances under which it would be right to mislead or deceive.

Daniel did not go to his home to pray so that he could hide. He did what he always did; verse 10 specifically makes this point. And he opened his windows towards Jerusalem not as an act of defiance but because this was his custom.

As a digression, it is worth thinking about that act. Why did he open his windows towards Jerusalem? There is no way that he could have seen more than a few miles, and probably not even that far in his eighties. Jerusalem was hundreds of miles away. But in his mind's eye, the only eyesight that actually improves with age, he could focus on Jerusalem and the temple – the place God had appointed to meet with man. Daniel's posture in prayer in captivity in a foreign land is precisely in accord with the terms of Solomon's prayer at the dedication of the temple in 1 Kings 8:47-49. We need to have a similar focus on Zion during the days of our pilgrimage in the lands of the Gentiles.

And what did he say in that prayer? The text in Daniel is moot as to the words he used. No doubt there would have been petitions regarding his current circumstances and the challenge that the king's decree presented. There also would have been a plea that God would bless His people Israel and restore again the kingdom to Israel. We may also be certain that the prayer included a call that God might bless Babylon with peace. In the very context of the Seventy Week prophecy Jeremiah had recorded God's instruction to the Israelites in captivity in Babylon to do just this:

> "Thus saith the LORD of hosts, the God of Israel, unto all that are carried away captives, whom I have caused to be carried

away from Jerusalem unto Babylon; Build ye houses, and dwell in them; and plant gardens, and eat the fruit of them; … and seek the peace of the city whither I have caused you to be carried away captives, and pray unto the LORD for it: for in the peace thereof shall ye have peace." (Jeremiah 29:4,5,7)

The same advice was given by Paul to saints in the first century:

"I exhort therefore, that, first of all, supplications, prayers, intercessions, and giving of thanks, be made for all men; for kings, and for all that are in authority; that we may lead a quiet and peaceable life in all godliness and honesty."

(1 Timothy 2:1,2)

Even when the saints are subject to laws which afflict or restrict them, they should pray for the governments that God has appointed to rule the nations in which they live. Peter exhorted the faithful in words which have remarkable parallels with the case of Daniel in Babylon:

"Dearly beloved, I beseech you as strangers and pilgrims, abstain from fleshly lusts, which war against the soul; having your conversation honest among the Gentiles: that, whereas they speak against you as evildoers, they may by your good works, which they shall behold, glorify God in the day of visitation. Submit yourselves to every ordinance of man for the Lord's sake: whether it be to the king, as supreme; or unto governors, as unto them that are sent by him for the punishment of evildoers, and for the praise of them that do well. For so is the will of God, that with well doing ye may put to silence the ignorance of foolish men: as free, and not using your liberty for a cloke of maliciousness, but as the servants of God. Honour all men. Love the brotherhood. Fear God. Honour the king." (1 Peter 2:11-17)

Daniel was a stranger and pilgrim, seeking to have his "conversation honest among the Gentiles" who sought to portray him as an evildoer. His objective was that, in spite of their antipathy, they might glorify God, as ultimately Darius did. Daniel would render honour to whom honour is due, in particular in this case Darius, but not at the expense of his own conscience.

Peter wrote these words from "Babylon" (1 Peter 5:13), which most commentators agree was code for Rome, reflecting the prophetical model under which Rome is the successor to Babylon in so many ways. The power of Peter's exhortation to "honour the king" is heightened when we take into account the fact that the king reigning in Rome at the time this was written was Nero, as corrupt and vile a ruler as ever ascended a throne. Nero aggressively persecuted the followers of Christ, but that in no way meant that the saints should not extend honour to him as their earthly king.

In Daniel 6:11-13 Daniel's opponents spring their trap and tell Darius that the prophet had disobeyed the decree. Darius is keen to deliver Daniel but finds himself also to have been trapped:

"Then these men assembled unto the king, and said unto the king, Know, O king, that the law of the Medes and Persians is, That no decree nor statute which the king establisheth may be changed."   (verse 15)

There was no way out for Darius or for Daniel, but in verse 16 the king had already realised the lesson that Nebuchadnezzar only learnt after he had sought to punish Daniel's friends:

"Then the king commanded, and they brought Daniel, and cast him into the den of lions. Now the king spake and said unto Daniel, Thy God whom thou servest continually, he will deliver thee."

The living God

Of course Daniel's God did indeed deliver him. Darius was troubled about Daniel's fate and when at last he came to enquire as to whether he had survived the ordeal he received Daniel's reassuring response:

"And when he came to the den, he cried with a lamentable voice unto Daniel: and the king spake and said to Daniel, O Daniel, servant of the living God, is thy God, whom thou servest continually, able to deliver thee from the lions? Then said Daniel unto the king, O king, live for ever. My God hath sent his angel, and hath shut the lions' mouths, that they have not hurt me: forasmuch as before him innocency was found in me; and also before thee, O king, have I done no hurt." (verses 20-22)

Darius' words in verse 20 are significant. He refers to Daniel's God as "the living God". This is a title that implies that all other gods are dead, powerless and ineffective. In the Bible it is a title used to denote the authority and superiority of the God of Israel.[11] He learnt an important lesson. Yahweh is now not just 'Daniel's God' as He had been in verse 16: He is now the one true Deity – the supreme divine authority. The faithfulness of the saints in the face of trial and even imprisonment can be a powerful testimony.

In verse 21 Daniel responded with the respect due to all rulers, even those who might persecute or imprison the saints. It was only after having offered that respect that he seeks in verse 22 to set the record straight. Daniel firstly declared that he had not transgressed the laws of God and only then added that he had also not done Darius any harm.

In verse 23 it is stated that Daniel was unharmed because "he believed in God". In this case Daniel's person was unharmed by the experience. For some brethren this has not been the case. Many have suffered injury and even death for the sake of the Gospel. But in a sense all have shared in Daniel's deliverance because they "believed in God", in that God will deliver them from the ultimate enemy of all the saints, from the power of sin and death.

The outcome of Daniel's ordeal in chapter 6 was remarkably similar to the case many years before in chapter 3. Another decree was issued to all men declaring the supremacy of Daniel's God:

"Then king Darius wrote unto all people, nations, and languages, that dwell in all the earth; Peace be multiplied unto you. I make a decree, That in every dominion of my kingdom men tremble and fear before the God of Daniel: for he is the living God, and stedfast for ever, and his kingdom that which

---

11 Examples include Joshua 3:10; 1 Samuel 17:26,36; 2 Kings 19:4,16 and Isaiah 37:4,17 (in 2 Kings 19 and Isaiah 37 the contrast is to the gods of Babylon).

shall not be destroyed, and his dominion shall be even unto the end. He delivereth and rescueth, and he worketh signs and wonders in heaven and in earth, who hath delivered Daniel from the power of the lions." (Daniel 6:25-27)

Darius, the most powerful human leader of his day, openly acknowledged the supremacy of "the God of Daniel"; he recognised that Israel's God is in control of all things. The structure of this record underlines that fact using an inverse pattern to emphasise that Almighty God alone controls the affairs of men:

A Action of the Crown – a new regime (verses 1-3);

  B Counteraction by the presidents – plotting against Daniel (verses 4-9);

    C Reaction of Daniel and Darius (verses 10-20);

      D Inaction – God is in control – the lions' mouths shut (verses 21,22);

    C Reaction of Darius and Daniel (verse 23);

  B Counteraction against the presidents and princes (verse 24);

A Action of the Crown – honours "the God of Daniel" (verses 25-27).

Darius' rule soon gave way to that of Cyrus, but the attitudes Darius expressed in this proclamation are reflected in the terms of Cyrus' decree in 536 BC calling for the rebuilding of the temple in Jerusalem as recorded in Ezra:

"Now in the first year of Cyrus king of Persia, that the word of the LORD by the mouth of Jeremiah might be fulfilled, the LORD stirred up the spirit of Cyrus king of Persia, that he made a proclamation throughout all his kingdom, and put it also in writing, saying, Thus saith Cyrus king of Persia, The LORD God of heaven hath given me all the kingdoms of the earth; and he hath charged me to build him an house at Jerusalem, which is in Judah. Who is there among you of all his people? his God be with him, and let him go up to Jerusalem, which is in Judah, and build the house of the LORD God of Israel, (he is the God,) which is in Jerusalem." (Ezra 1:1-3)

Of course, as was the case previously, the lesson Darius learnt and which Cyrus also accepted slipped from the consciousness of the nations and they returned to their old ways. It has ever been thus. But ultimately this lesson will be learnt by the nations when the Lord Jesus Christ establishes the kingdom of God and all nations will flow up to Jerusalem.

We long for that time. In the meantime we seek to maintain a steadfast walk with our gaze, like that of Daniel, fixed upon Jerusalem. We must maintain our service before Almighty God and endure the challenges that come upon us from the world – whether they take the form of the informal trials and temptations that come from the people around us, or whether they are manifested in more organised opposition from the authorities God has ordained in the nations of this age.

5 |

Peter – obeying God rather than men

DISCIPLESHIP always comes at a price. We have seen that in the case of faithful Israelites as recorded in the Old Testament. The same is true in the New Testament.

John the Baptist's bold preaching was an implicit challenge to the effete Jewish leadership, both secular and religious. His preaching in the wilderness helped to shield him to some degree from the wrath of the authorities, but he stepped on too many influential toes when he criticised Herod Antipas for entering into an immoral marriage:

"Herod himself had sent forth and laid hold upon John, and bound him in prison for Herodias' sake, his brother Philip's wife: for he had married her. For John had said unto Herod, It is not lawful for thee to have thy brother's wife."

(Mark 6:17,18)

The Law of Moses was clear: Leviticus 18:16 strictly prohibited a man from taking his brother's wife while his brother was still alive. Herod Antipas, however, became obsessed by his half-brother Philip's wife, divorced his first wife and married her. John the Baptist could not countenance such a gross breach of God's laws and spoke out, incurring the wrath of Herodias.

To placate her, Herod imprisoned John, but that did not satisfy his ambitious and vindictive wife. Nothing short of John's execution would assuage her hatred of this man of God who had so openly condemned her evil behaviour. Her husband, however, had a measure of respect for John and even found him intriguing.

This made Herod reluctant to execute what he knew to be "a just man", even if he had criticised him:

> "Herodias had a grudge against him and wanted to put him to death. But she could not, for Herod feared John, knowing that he was a righteous and holy man, and he kept him safe. When he heard him, he was greatly perplexed, and yet he heard him gladly."   (Mark 6:19,20, ESV)

It has often been the case that secular authorities have had respect for the moral integrity of conscientious objectors who have made a stand for what they believe to be the will of God. This has led them to be generous in their treatment of them, even if they have been obliged to impinge upon their liberty. An example of this is the way in which many young brothers who were granted exemption from military service during periods of conscription received very considerate treatment when being required to engage in work of national importance.

Not all conscientious objectors received such generous treatment, however, and corrupt officials have been known to look for ways to make their situation difficult. Few, though, have had to face the wrath of a woman like Herodias. A rash vow by her intoxicated husband at his birthday banquet gave Herodias the opportunity she had been waiting for; she seized on it and John the Baptist was beheaded forthwith (verses 21-28).

The example of the Lord Jesus

The pre-eminent example of one who suffered for making a stand for the things of God is, of course, our Lord and saviour himself. Arrested in the dead of night to avoid risking an adverse reaction by a fickle crowd, he was crucified by "wicked hands" (Acts 2:23). Several times he had warned his disciples that he would be arrested and put to death by the Jewish rulers. Immediately prior to the transfiguration the Lord had sought to warn his disciples of what was ahead in language which is unambiguous:

> "From that time forth began Jesus to shew unto his disciples, how that he must go unto Jerusalem, and suffer many things

of the elders and chief priests and scribes, and be killed, and
be raised again the third day." (Matthew 16:21)

Matthew's phrase "from that time forth" indicates this was
a point Jesus would repeatedly seek to impress upon his disciples.
We see evidence of this in the very next chapter, when he raises
the issue in verses 9-12,22,23. The record shows, however, that
on every occasion, in spite of the very blunt way in which the
Lord spoke, the disciples failed to grasp the significance of his
words.

In some of these statements the Lord makes explicit
reference to the fact that, having been executed, he would rise
again on the third day. It is clear from their bewilderment when
their Master was crucified and their astonishment when he was
resurrected that the disciples had not comprehended what their
Lord was telling them so plainly. Given this fact, we can only
wonder how much they appreciated the personal significance
of this statement which he made when he first imparted this
message to his disciples:

"Then said Jesus unto his disciples, If any man will come after
me, let him deny himself, and take up his cross, and follow
me." (Matthew 16:24)

Those who wish to be glorified with the Lord Jesus Christ must
also be willing to suffer with him. They might not have to face
literal crucifixion, but they do have to put to death the old man;
they do have to be "crucified with Christ" (Galatians 2:20).

The disciples' stand

After the Lord's resurrection, the disciples who had not
understood the full significance of these statements previously
soon came to appreciate what this meant, not just for their
Lord but for themselves also. Jesus commissioned his disciples
to preach the Gospel "in Jerusalem, and in all Judaea, and in
Samaria, and unto the uttermost part of the earth" (Acts 1:8). In
response to this command they started as directed in Jerusalem,
in the process invoking quite early the wrath of the Jewish
leaders, the very men who had conspired against their Lord

and Master. The anger of the Jewish leaders is hardly surprising given the remarkable response to their first preaching campaign at Pentecost as recorded in Acts 2, when about three thousand embraced the message they proclaimed.

Peter and John continued to create a stir by teaching in the temple courts. In response, the Jewish officials arrested them and held them in custody overnight (Acts 4:3) with a view to questioning them in the morning. The next day a formidable host of the Jewish elite gathered to interrogate Peter and John:

"It came to pass on the morrow, that their rulers, and elders, and scribes, and Annas the high priest, and Caiaphas, and John, and Alexander, and as many as were of the kindred of the high priest, were gathered together at Jerusalem. And when they had set them in the midst, they asked, By what power, or by what name, have ye done this?"   (Acts 4:5,6)

This was a 'who's who' of the Jewish ruling class. Unquestionably the vast number involved was designed to intimidate Peter and John, who they appear to have regarded as simple, rustic Galileans (the record goes on in verse 13 to refer to their astonishment at the confidence of these "unlearned and ignorant men"). Given the experiences that Peter and John had been through with Jesus, however, they were not to be cowed by these angry men, even if they were the very ones who had conspired against their Master.

When making a stand as a conscientious objector, many a brother or sister has had to confront powerful officials and give an account of their beliefs and actions. It can be intimidating, especially if the officials are more articulate and better educated than the one being examined, as was the case with Peter and John in Acts 4. As daunting as it can be, however, they should take heart that it will be evident to their interrogators that "they had been with Jesus" (Acts 4:13). A believer may not be a gifted orator but if he or she speaks from the heart of the things which they believe it will be a compelling testimony. Magistrates who have examined conscientious objectors have commented that they were not particularly interested in whether a logically compelling, scripturally watertight case was made for the position held, but rather that the applicants conscientiously believed in the course of action they felt obliged to adopt. Erudition is of little consequence; what matters most is conviction.

Peter and John were commanded that should cease preaching about Jesus. Like Daniel's friends before Nebuchadnezzar, they responded politely but unflinchingly:

"Whether it be right in the sight of God to hearken unto you more than unto God, judge ye. For we cannot but speak the things which we have seen and heard."   (verses 19,20)

Jeremiah found he could not suppress the divine message which was a fire in his bones (Jeremiah 20:9); Peter, John and the other apostles likewise were unable to keep silent. The leaders threatened them further but let them go. They left and continued to preach, in spite of the injunction imposed by the rulers. That preaching continued to win many converts, "multitudes both of men and women" (Acts 5:14).

This continuing success provoked the rulers to intervene again:

"Then the high priest rose up, and all they that were with him (which is the sect of the Sadducees), and were filled with indignation, and laid their hands on the apostles, and put them in the common prison."   (verses 17,18)

Previously when they had been held in custody overnight, presumably in the temple precincts, there was no reference to a prison. Now they are despatched as common criminals to the public prison. Like the prison in which Joseph was detained, this would have been a most unpleasant place, but unlike Joseph they were not there long before an angel delivered them from incarceration (verse 19). This angel, acting as the agent of God, commanded them to do exactly the opposite of what the rulers had instructed them to do – to go to the temple and preach the word (verse 20). They had no choice other than to obey.

When the rulers realised that not only had the apostles managed to leave the prison, but that also they were openly preaching in the name of Jesus in the temple, they were outraged.

Once again they brought the apostles before the combined Jewish leadership and harangued them:

> "We strictly charged you not to teach in this name, yet here you have filled Jerusalem with your teaching, and you intend to bring this man's blood upon us." (verse 28, ESV)

They had, in fact, brought his blood upon themselves, for they had knowingly put to death an innocent man, but inconvenient facts mean little to corrupt officials.

We can hear the vitriol in their words, but again the apostles are not intimidated and their response is one of the cornerstone passages for all believers who are required to make a stand for their conscience:

> "Then Peter and the other apostles answered and said, We ought to obey God rather than men." (verse 29)

Provocatively, Peter (who appears to be the spokesman here) illustrated the principle by pointing out that God had raised up Jesus but that they had refused to accept him (verse 30). The rulers might be willing to flout the will of God but the apostles would never willingly disobey their God.

The servants of God are commanded to respect the secular authorities and comply with the laws of the land in which they live (Romans 13:1-7). Jesus himself instructed the people, including his disciples, to obey the very rulers who were now challenging those same disciples:

> "Then spake Jesus to the multitude, and to his disciples, saying, The scribes and the Pharisees sit in Moses' seat: all therefore whatsoever they bid you observe, that observe and do; but do not ye after their works: for they say, and do not." (Matthew 23:1-3)

But what if the authorities command the disciples of Jesus to do that which is contrary to God's will and the commandments of their Lord? Clearly their first allegiance must be to their heavenly King and the will of God must prevail regardless of the cost. As was the case with Daniel and his friends in Babylon, the apostles had no choice but to refuse the demand of the rulers so that they could remain faithful to the commandments of God.

And just as had been the case in Nebuchadnezzar's court, the boldness of the apostles enraged the rulers even further, and they "took counsel to slay them" (Acts 5:33). The noted scholar Gamaliel urged a less extreme response and this prevailed at the time, although they still beat the apostles before releasing them.

The apostles went forth bruised but unbroken and continued to preach. The murderous intent of the more hostile rulers was manifested a short time later when Stephen was stoned for daring to challenge them. After this, Paul afflicted the early Christians, but following his conversion the ecclesia seems to have enjoyed some respite from the harassment that had been so constant.

Peter delivered from prison

That respite was not to last, however, and Peter and the other apostles again fell foul of the authorities in Acts 12. Herod executed James, the brother of John, and arrested and imprisoned Peter (verses 2-4). This Herod is Herod Agrippa I, grandson of Herod the Great who had slaughtered the young boys in Bethlehem, and the brother of Herodias who had been responsible for the beheading of John the Baptist (Mark 6:14-29). He was a strict observer of the Law of Moses, which coupled with the family's propensity for extreme violence made him a very real threat to the followers of Christ.

The reference in Acts 12:2 to killing James with the sword suggests that, like John the Baptist, James may have been beheaded. Although it cannot be relied upon as absolutely certain, Eusebius makes reference to the earlier testimony of Clement that:

> "The man who led him [James] to the judgement seat, seeing him bearing his testimony to the faith, and moved by the fact, confessed himself a Christian. Both, therefore, says he, were led away to die."[1]

1   *Eusebius*, Book 2.9.

Whether or not this record is accurate, the fact remains that those taking a stand for their belief in Christ can have a powerful and at times life changing impact on those around them through their steadfastness in the face of trial. This was seen in the case of Nebuchadnezzar in Daniel 3 and Darius in Daniel 6, and it may well have been the case here with James.

We know for certain that there were some who were very impressed by the slaying of James, but for less noble reasons. The Jewish officials were pleased to see one of their opponents put to death and Herod, always keen to garner support wherever he could, decided to build on this goodwill by seizing Peter. There are times, especially under corrupt regimes or during times of crisis, when the believers can become the victims of stringent measures because it will please another group. Thus it is that some brothers, when seeking exemption from military service, have sometimes been pilloried and vilified by magistrates and in the media, especially during times when the country in which they were pilgrims and strangers has been severely threatened.

Knowing of James' fate, one can only imagine the trepidation Peter must have felt as he was taken off to prison for the second time. Until now the apostles had been able to walk amidst the furnace of persecution but "the fire had no power, nor was an hair of their head singed, neither were their coats changed, nor the smell of fire had passed on them" (Daniel 3:27). Stephen had been killed and Paul refers to other believers being executed (Acts 26:10), but this was the first time such extreme action had been taken against one of the apostles themselves; now one of the leading apostles is executed and another is imprisoned to await execution.

One of the hardest lessons of all for disciples to learn is the fact that, while God promises to be with them and to deliver them, that does not mean they will never suffer calamity. Many terrible afflictions may well come upon them, but they will be delivered:

> "The righteous cry, and the LORD heareth, and delivereth them out of all their troubles. The LORD is nigh unto them

that are of a broken heart; and saveth such as be of a contrite spirit. Many are the afflictions of the righteous: but the LORD delivereth him out of them all." (Psalm 34:17-19)

For James, deliverance would be at the resurrection of the dead. Peter would experience a more immediate, if less permanent, deliverance, but he was unaware of that fact as he languished in prison during the Passover celebrations.

No doubt aware that Peter had somehow managed to escape from prison earlier, Herod took no chances. He appointed four quaternions (Greek, *tetradion*) to guard Peter. A quaternion is a group of four soldiers who work as a team to guard a prisoner, with two soldiers being chained to the prisoner while the other two keep watch, as per the description in Acts 12:6. As the night was divided into four watches, four groups of four were required to ensure that Peter had no chance of escape – or so Herod hoped!

Peter was the subject of prayer by his brothers and sisters. He would have expected that and would draw strength from the fact. In these more stringent circumstances, what Peter would not have expected was a further angelic deliverance from prison. The text indicates that Peter actually doubted what was transpiring (verse 9) even as the deliverance was unfolding! We are not always conscious of how God will deliver us from the trials we face, and sometimes deliverance will come in ways we could never have anticipated. Whatever our circumstances, however, we may be certain that we will be delivered.

"Be not conformed to this world"

In the light of Peter's example of repeated sufferings at the hands of both religious and secular authorities, his advice to the first century Christians in 1 Peter 2 is especially powerful:

"Beloved, I urge you as sojourners and exiles to abstain from the passions of the flesh, which wage war against your soul. Keep your conduct among the Gentiles honourable, so that when they speak against you as evildoers, they may see your good deeds and glorify God on the day of visitation. Be subject for the Lord's sake to every human institution, whether it be to the emperor as supreme, or to governors as sent by him to punish those who do evil and to praise those who do good. For this is the will of God, that by doing good you should put to silence the ignorance of foolish people. Live as people who are free, not using your freedom as a cover-up for evil, but living as servants of God. Honour everyone. Love the brotherhood. Fear God. Honour the emperor." (1 Peter 2:11-17, ESV)

Sometimes first century brothers and sisters, as conscientious objectors, suffered persecution because they would not conform to those requirements of the state which conflicted with their obligations as servants of God. That was the case with Peter and the other apostles when the Jewish rulers ordered them to desist from preaching about Jesus Christ. At other times, they were the victims of malicious rulers whose malice was exacerbated by what they perceived to be the anti-social behaviour and attitudes of men and women who stood apart, heeding the advice that they "be not conformed to this world" (Romans 12:2), which might well have been the case with James and Peter in Acts 12.

When large parts of Rome were engulfed in fire during the tenth year of Nero's reign it was rumoured that the emperor himself was the arsonist responsible. To divert suspicion the emperor had to find a scapegoat, which he found in the followers of Christ living in the city. The Roman historian Tacitus' record of the sufferings of Christians under Nero is interesting, both for the way it picks up the language of Hebrews 11 and for the light it sheds on the words of Peter in 1 Peter 2:

"He inflicted the most exquisite tortures on those men, who, under the vulgar appellation of Christians, were already branded with deserved infamy. They derived their name and origin from Christ, who in the reign of Tiberius had suffered death by the sentence of the procurator Pontius Pilate. For a while this dire superstition was checked; but it again burst forth; and not only spread itself over Judea, the first seat of this mischievous sect, but was even introduced into Rome, the common asylum which receives and protects whatever is impure, whatever is atrocious. The confessions of those who were seized discovered a great multitude of their accomplices, and they were all convicted, not so much for the crime of setting fire to the city, as for their hatred of human kind. They died in torments, and their torments were embittered by insult and derision. Some were nailed on crosses; others sewn up in the skins of wild beasts, and exposed to the fury of dogs; others again, smeared over with combustible materials, were used as torches to illuminate the darkness of the night. The gardens of Nero were destined for the melancholy spectacle, which was accompanied with a horse race and honoured with the presence of the emperor, who mingled with the populace in the dress and attitude of a charioteer. The guilt of the Christians deserved indeed the most exemplary punishment, but the public abhorrence was changed into commiseration, from the opinion that those unhappy wretches were sacrificed, not so much to the public welfare, as to the cruelty of a jealous tyrant."[2]

Tacitus points out that people spoke ill of the Christians, accusing them of a "hatred of human kind", in spite of the fact that they did nothing to warrant such a claim. Peter says that he was writing from "Babylon" (1 Peter 5:13), which is believed to be a code name for Rome; Nero was emperor of Rome at that time. In spite of the vile way in which Nero treated the Christians of the very city in which he was then residing, Peter's advice is that they should "honour the emperor".

When Edward Gibbon quotes this extract from Tacitus he draws attention to the curious fact that the Circus Vaticanus, the site of Nero's palace garden where some of the persecution described by Tacitus took place, later became the site for the headquarters of the Roman Catholic system:

"Those who survey with a curious eye the revolutions of mankind, may observe, that the gardens and circus of Nero on the Vatican, which were polluted with the blood of the

---

2   Tacitus, *Annals*, XV. 44.

first Christians, have been rendered still more famous by the triumph and by the abuse of the persecuted religion. On the same spot, a temple [i.e., St. Peter's Basilica], which far surpasses the ancient glories of the Capitol, has been since erected by the Christian Pontiffs, who, deriving their claim of universal dominion from an humble fisherman of Galilee, have succeeded to the throne of the Caesars, given laws to the barbarian conquerors of Rome, and extended their spiritual jurisdiction from the coast of the Baltic to the shores of the Pacific Ocean."[3]

It is indeed much more than curious that this centre for the persecution of early Christians should later become the site of the headquarters of the Roman Catholic Church, a system which would arrest, imprison and execute so many who embraced the hope of Israel in later centuries. It is further incidental evidence of this system's position as the continuation of the Roman power.

The heritage of this site may be seen in several aspects of the Roman Catholic system. The Vatican Hill is not one of the famous "seven hills of Rome". It is, in fact, on the opposite side of the River Tiber from the seven hills. In addition to being the site of the circus of Nero, it was the location of the Phrygianum, a temple of the goddess Cybele. Romans referred to Cybele as Magna Mater (Great Mother), or as Magna Mater deorum Idaea (great Idaean mother of the gods). The priests who served Cybele, known as Galli, were emasculated and relied on the generosity of devotees of the goddess to support them. It was not uncommon in ancient times for men to be emasculated by brutal overlords, especially if they were captured in war. For example, it is very likely that Daniel and his friends were treated in this way by the Babylonians. The priests of Cybele, however, chose to be emasculated. It was thought that the voluntary emasculation of the Galli in their devotion to the goddess gave them powers of prophecy. The parallels between the Galli of Cybele and the prelates of the later Roman Catholic system are extraordinary.

3   Edward Gibbon, *Decline and Fall of the Roman Empire*, chapter 16.

These successors of Nero and his regime would continue to persecute the followers of Christ while ever and wherever they had the capacity to do so, but the deliverance that God promises all his saints would also continue.

"Follow me"

Peter was delivered from prison and, while the Acts record after chapter 12 focuses primarily on the work of Paul and his colleagues in Gentile lands, we see a glimpse of Peter's work in Jerusalem in Acts 15, after which he seems to fade from the record. What became of him? Church tradition says that he was crucified upside down outside Rome about twenty-five years after his Lord had been crucified. The Bible is silent about that, but it does record a prophecy of the Lord which suggests that he may have been executed (as suggested by the use of the word "death" in John 21:19). It certainly indicates that he would at least be held against his will:

> "Verily, verily, I say unto thee, When thou wast young, thou girdedst thyself, and walkedst whither thou wouldest: but when thou shalt be old, thou shalt stretch forth thy hands, and another shall gird thee, and carry thee whither thou wouldest not. This spake he, signifying by what death he should glorify God. And when he had spoken this, he saith unto him, Follow me."   (John 21:18,19)

"Follow me": it is a command designed to evoke memories of earlier words spoken by Jesus in Peter's hearing.

Peter had sought to deter his Master from being taken prisoner and allowing himself to be crucified. Now, upon hearing this ominous prediction of what awaited him, a converted Peter shows no concern or reticence. Rather than expressing concern for himself, his response is to ask what would be the fate of his friend John (verse 21). The Lord's reply does not answer Peter's question: the circumstances of other disciples is irrelevant in relation of our discipleship. What matters is how each of us responds to the vicissitudes of our life in Christ, not what good or evil may befall others.

As it happened, John would also one day be carried to somewhere he did not wish to go. Under the reign of Domitian, John would be exiled to the isle of Patmos because of his faithfulness to "the word of God, and for the testimony of Jesus Christ" (Revelation 1:9). But that was not relevant, and our Lord seeks to correct Peter's perspective:

"Jesus saith unto him, If I will that he tarry till I come, what is that to thee? follow thou me."   (John 21:22)

Along with his fellow disciples, Peter had been slow to grasp the meaning of the Lord's words when he had tried to prepare his disciples for what was to transpire in Jerusalem. Having witnessed the arrest of his Lord and seen him raised from the tomb, Peter views things very differently. Most importantly, he has grasped the significance of words his Master had used in conjunction with references to his forthcoming death:

"If any man will come after me, let him deny himself, and take up his cross, and follow me."   (Matthew 16:24)

"Follow me." Peter did just that, taking up his cross, following his Master in denying himself, preaching the Gospel and suffering arrest for his faithfulness to the will of God. Whether the tradition is true that he also was literally crucified we cannot be sure, but we do know that in his last recorded letter to his brothers and sisters he wrote these words in which he refers to his imminent death:

"Yea, I think it meet, as long as I am in this tabernacle, to stir you up by putting you in remembrance; knowing that shortly I must put off this my tabernacle, even as our Lord Jesus Christ hath shewed me. Moreover I will endeavour that ye may be able after my decease to have these things always in remembrance. For we have not followed cunningly devised fables, when we made known unto you the power and coming of our Lord Jesus Christ, but were eyewitnesses of his majesty. For he received from God the Father honour and glory, when there came such a voice to him from the excellent glory, This is my beloved Son, in whom I am well pleased. And this voice which came from heaven we heard, when we were with him in the holy mount." (2 Peter 1:13-18)

Perhaps Peter already was a prisoner when he penned this exhortation. If not, the day would soon come for him to be held against his will – but what would that matter? It is both poignant and significant that in this final message Peter alludes to his presence, together with James and John, on the mount of transfiguration when both the Lord Jesus and his disciples were encouraged in their preparation for what Jesus was to endure in Jerusalem. So Peter closes his ministry as a follower of the Lord, exhorting his fellow followers to endure whatever might befall them as they await the glory and majesty of the age to come.

6 |

Paul – "in prisons more frequent"

P ETER'S faithfulness came at a cost. From Paul, discipleship
also extracted a particularly high price:
"Are they ministers of Christ? (I speak as a fool) I am
more; in labours more abundant, in stripes above measure,
in prisons more frequent, in deaths oft. Of the Jews five
times received I forty stripes save one. Thrice was I beaten
with rods, once was I stoned, thrice I suffered shipwreck, a
night and a day I have been in the deep; in journeyings often,
in perils of waters, in perils of robbers, in perils by mine own
countrymen, in perils by the heathen, in perils in the city, in
perils in the wilderness, in perils in the sea, in perils among
false brethren; in weariness and painfulness, in watchings
often, in hunger and thirst, in fastings often, in cold and
nakedness. Beside those things that are without, that
which cometh upon me daily, the care of all the ecclesias."

(2 Corinthians 11:23-28)

Not all of these trials are recorded explicitly in the New
Testament, but many are.

Saul of Tarsus, who we meet for the first time in Acts 7:58,
was a gifted man. He was born a Roman citizen in the prosperous
trading city of Tarsus. We may presume from the fact he was sent
to Jerusalem for his education that his family were both religious
and well off. His father was a Pharisee (Acts 23:6) who wanted
his son to be brought up in the strictest traditions of that sect.
To that end he studied in Jerusalem at the feet of Gamaliel, "a

teacher of the law held in honour by all the people" (Acts 5:34, ESV).

Saul the persecutor

From the perspective of a first century Pharisee, Saul had the world at his feet. It would seem Saul was eager to make his mark early and that might explain his virulent campaign against the followers of Christ. Unfortunately, while he was a diligent student of the laws and traditions of the Jews as taught by Gamaliel, Saul did not take heed of his tutor's attitude towards the Christians. When Peter was brought before the council in Acts 5, Gamaliel argued for restraint when dealing with the followers of Jesus:

> "Ye men of Israel, take heed to yourselves what ye intend to do as touching these men ... I say unto you, Refrain from these men, and let them alone: for if this counsel or this work be of men, it will come to nought: but if it be of God, ye cannot overthrow it; lest haply ye be found even to fight against God."   (Acts 5:35,38,39)

This entirely reasonable (if perhaps disingenuous) counsel could be expected to have only a very limited impact on men who had willingly and knowingly put to death their own Messiah. Presumably his standing helped him to carry the argument on the day. While the Jewish leaders allowed themselves to be influenced by this logic at least for a short time, unfortunately, his protégé Saul of Tarsus did not heed Gamaliel's advice.

In his zeal to resist the inexorable progress of the Gospel message being preached by the apostles, Saul "made havok of the ecclesia, entering into every house, and haling men and women committed them to prison" (Acts 8:3; see also Acts 22:4). His fanaticism was not bound by gender – men and women alike were thrown into prison for daring to declare faith in the Lord Jesus Christ. Saul even spoke in favour of the death penalty for believers in Christ (Acts 26:10).

The record in Acts shows that this persecution became a catalyst for the spreading of the Gospel to new fields (Acts 8:4), which accords with the sentiments of Romans 8:28, "that all things work together for good to them that love God, to them who are the called according to his purpose". It certainly was not Saul's intention that he should facilitate the spread of the good news concerning the kingdom of God and the name of Jesus Christ, but nonetheless that was the consequence of his enmity towards Christ and those who followed him.

This firebrand from Tarsus was not one to be thwarted in his endeavours. If the followers of Christ were going to disperse to escape his fury he would take his fury to them. Thus Acts 9 opens with Saul "breathing out threatenings and slaughter against the disciples of the Lord" (verse 1) and obtaining from the High Priest a mandate to extend his programme of persecution to the Jewish community in Damascus. It was his intent that any he found in that city that were "of the way" (KJV margin) were to be brought "bound" to Jerusalem (verse 2), where no doubt they would join their fellow believers in prison.

The prisoner of Christ

Saul's conversion on the Damascus road brought an end to his virulent persecution of the ecclesia. Saul's name was changed to Paul as he underwent fundamental change in every other respect. From being one who imprisoned those who were members of the body of Christ, he becomes the prisoner of Christ (Ephesians 3:1; 4:1, 2 Timothy 1:8; Philemon 1,9). The Greek word translated "prisoner" (*desmios*) occurs sixteen times in the New Testament. Only three specific men are identified by this word: twelve occurrences of the term refer to Paul (two of which include Silas as a fellow prisoner),[1] while three refer to Barabbas. One can only speculate what Paul thought of this (apparently) undesigned alignment between himself and the brigand who had been released at the expense of his innocent Lord.

There is one generic use of the word *desmios* in the New Testament. In Hebrews 13 the saints are exhorted to:

1　The other references to Paul individually as a prisoner are in Acts 23:18; 25:14,27; 28:16,17.

"Remember prisoners, as if you were in prison with them; and
remember those suffering ill-treatment, for you yourselves
also are still in the body."   (verse 3, Weymouth)

When we concern ourselves with the needs of those
imprisoned, especially those who are incarcerated for their
commitment to God's will, we might ponder how our actions
will be viewed by our Lord who, in the parable of the sheep and
the goats, commended those who came to him when he was
in prison, which they did by doing it to one of the least of his
brethren (Matthew 25:34-40).

Along with Barnabas, on his first missionary journey Paul
preached boldly in Pisidian Antioch. This preaching appealed to
some of the Gentile hearers but antagonised many of the Jewish
leaders (Acts 13:48-50). Following their Lord's advice in Luke 9:5
"they shook off the dust of their feet" and moved on to new fields.
Acts 14 records Paul's work with Barnabas in Iconium, Lystra,
Derbe and Perga and his return to Antioch in Syria. A feature of
this record is the persecution Paul and Barnabas experienced.

Firstly, in Iconium Paul's initial success generated hostility
from "unbelieving Jews":

"But the unbelieving Jews stirred up the Gentiles, and made
their minds evil affected against the brethren."   (Acts 14:2)

In verse 5 we see that they worked with the local Gentiles to
threaten Paul:

"And when there was an assault made both of the Gentiles,
and also of the Jews with their rulers, to use them despitefully,
and to stone them, They were ware of it, and fled unto Lystra
and Derbe, cities of Lycaonia, and unto the region that
lieth round about: and there they preached the gospel."

(verses 5-7)

Our Lord's recommendation to his disciples was, "when
they persecute you in this city, flee ye into another" (Matthew
10:23). That advice was taken by Paul, and it remains sound advice
for the prisoners of Christ today. Paul was being threatened
because of his stand for the things of God. He could have stayed
to confront his adversaries, but God provided a means of avoiding

conflict and he took advantage of that. In our own lives there will be times when our conscience brings us into conflict with others and it is not wrong to 'flee to another place' if that avenue is available without our compromising our conscience.

Paul and his companions moved on to Derbe and Lystra and preached the Gospel in those cities. At Lystra he created quite a stir. In fact, Paul struggled to contain the extreme enthusiasm of the locals, at least until subversive Jews arrived to turn the people against him. At Iconium Paul had found a means of escaping persecution but there was no avenue of escape on this occasion:

> "There came thither certain Jews from Antioch and Iconium, who persuaded the people, and, having stoned Paul, drew him out of the city, supposing he had been dead."   (Acts 14:19)

When his servants make a stand for their conscience there are times when God allows them an avenue of escape. At other times they must face the consequences of their beliefs. At Iconium Paul was spared the violence his opponents planned to inflict; in Lystra he had to endure suffering for conscience sake. Although the murderous intent of his opponents is clear from the text, through the mercy of God Paul was spared and in verse 20 he rose and subsequently moved on to Derbe.

In this one chapter Paul goes through almost the full gamut of the experiences of a conscientious objector. He is threatened with adverse consequences for his stand and is delivered from them, but later he suffers severely for making a stand. Regardless of the outcome, however, Paul was not dissuaded from following his conscience.

Paul's refusal to cower in the face of hostility is evident from the fact that, after the Jerusalem Conference (Acts 15), accompanied by Silas he commenced his second missionary journey with a visit to Lystra, the very city in which he had been stoned (Acts 16:1). On that occasion Paul was not harmed and he moved on, eventually crossing the Aegean Sea and arriving in Philippi.

Further persecution

In Philippi Paul again suffered persecution for the sake of the Gospel:

> "The multitude rose up together against them: and the magistrates rent off their clothes, and commanded to beat them. And when they had laid many stripes upon them, they cast them into prison, charging the jailor to keep them safely: who, having received such a charge, thrust them into the inner prison, and made their feet fast in the stocks."

(Acts 16:22-24)

Paul and Silas were not only beaten. Like Joseph, Jeremiah, Daniel and his friends before him, they became prisoners of conscience. And like Joseph and Jeremiah, to add to their suffering and ignominy, their legs were confined. Verse 26 refers to the miraculous loosing of their bands, which may suggest that they also were bound with chains.

What did it mean to be placed in stocks? There was one form of stocks which made provision for the binding of both legs, both arms and the neck. This is the kind of stocks most often depicted in pictures of Protestants who were persecuted by the Roman Catholic Church in the Middle Ages. The text, however, mentions only their feet being constricted, and there were stocks that took the form of a wooden bar that constrained only the legs.

The Greek word translated stocks is *xulon*, which just means wood. This word occurs nineteen times in the New Testament; four of these are in Acts. Curiously, in every other instance in Acts where this word is used, it refers to the cross upon which our Lord Jesus Christ was crucified (Acts 5:30; 10:39; 13:29). Paul would use the word himself to refer to the tree upon which his Lord was crucified (Galatians 3:13); Peter likewise employed the word to refer to the cross (1 Peter 2:24). The apostle who would say to the Galatians, "I am crucified with Christ" (Galatians 2:20) may well have seen in this experience an earnest of what it is to "fill up that which is behind of the afflictions of Christ in my flesh for his body's sake, which is the ecclesia" (Colossians 1:24).

The Greek *xulon* is used in other contexts which also are significant:

- Five times the word is used to refer to the staves with which the mob who arrested Jesus were armed (Matthew 26:47,55; Mark 14:43,48; Luke 22:52).
- It is used by the Lord to describe himself as a "green tree" when he was being crucified (Luke 23:31).
- Four times it is used when referring to the "tree of life" (Revelation 2:7; 22:2 [twice]; 22:14).

Surely Paul and Silas would see in this instrument of torture and confinement a link to the suffering of their Lord and also a link to the great deliverance that is promised for all who are held in bondage to the law of sin and death.

Did Paul and Silas complain that God had deserted them, that God had let them down? Did they recant and abandon their principles? No, they bore the price of making a stand for God with dignity and calm assurance. In fact, Acts 16:25 says they praised God. Here is the assurance of faith: a faith that knows, regardless of our circumstances, we are never alone or forsaken; a faith that knows God can and will deliver His servants, even though we might not always appreciate how.

The example of Paul and Silas in meekly enduring the indignity heaped upon them had a profound effect on the Philippian jailer, who responded to "the word of the Lord" they spoke when explaining the way of salvation. Thus it has been in the case of others who have suffered. Pharaoh's butler remembered Joseph's faithfulness, albeit belatedly, and both Nebuchadnezzar and Darius changed their views when impressed by the faithfulness of Daniel and his friends when they made a stand for their conscience. There have been similar examples in modern times of observers being motivated to consider the beliefs of brothers and sisters who have been prepared to pay the price that faithfulness to God has demanded when the requirements of the state or of their employer were in conflict with the commandments of God.

Having converted the jailer and his family, Paul and Silas were delivered the following day and moved on to Thessalonica. In this city they also experienced hostility (Acts 17:5-9), so they moved on to Berea. Verse 13 reveals their opponents followed them from Thessalonica and stirred up animosity in Berea too. While some like the Philippian jailer may be moved by our stand and conduct, we should not expect our adversaries to let up in their opposition to the Gospel and, like Paul, we must not let up in our stand for the Gospel.

From Berea, Paul moved on to Athens, Corinth and then Ephesus without experiencing a serious threat to his safety. Acts 19 records that Paul's preaching provoked a riot in Ephesus, but again God delivered him. In due course Paul travelled to Jerusalem to celebrate the feast of Pentecost. While en route in Acts 21 he passed through Caesarea, where he encountered a prophet named Agabus who prophesied that Paul faced arrest if he continued with his plan to go to Jerusalem:

"As we tarried there many days, there came down from Judaea a certain prophet, named Agabus. And when he was come unto us, he took Paul's girdle, and bound his own hands and feet, and said, Thus saith the Holy Spirit, So shall the Jews at Jerusalem bind the man that owneth this girdle, and shall deliver him into the hands of the Gentiles. And when we heard these things, both we, and they of that place, besought him not to go up to Jerusalem. Then Paul answered, What mean ye to weep and to break mine heart? for I am ready not to be bound only, but also to die at Jerusalem for the name of the Lord Jesus."   (Acts 21:10-13)

Agabus was right, and Paul did not doubt his words. But, like his Master the Lord Jesus Christ, Paul had set his face steadfastly toward Jerusalem. As in the case of his Lord, it was the will of God that Paul proceed, and he was prepared to face the consequences of his convictions.

Paul travelled to Jerusalem where he was the subject of a false accusation, just like Joseph, Jeremiah, Daniel's friends and our Lord Jesus Christ. The Jews conspired against him, just as they had conspired against Jesus, but Paul used his Roman citizenship to appeal to the Roman overlords.

It may seem a little odd that Paul invoked his Roman citizenship. His real citizenship, after all, was in heaven; he was a subject of the kingdom of God, and merely a stranger and pilgrim in so far as worldly affairs were concerned. There is nothing wrong, however, with taking advantage of the circumstances in which we find ourselves so long as we may do so without compromising our conscience. We are to obey God rather than man when there is a conflict between the commandments of God and the expectations of the authorities God has ordained to rule the nations. But where there is no conflict, we are to be peaceable and law-abiding and may take advantage of the protection the authorities offer.

To Rome for trial

So it was that Paul became a prisoner of the Romans. He did not stop preaching, even while a prisoner. But was he really a prisoner of Rome? Not really. When Paul eventually was taken to Rome for trial he was established in his own house where he preached to any who visited him. The leaders of the Jewish community in Rome came to see Paul and he eloquently set out his circumstances:

> "It came to pass, that after three days Paul called the chief of the Jews together: and when they were come together, he said unto them, Men and brethren, though I have committed nothing against the people, or customs of our fathers, yet was I delivered prisoner from Jerusalem into the hands of the Romans. Who, when they had examined me, would have let me go, because there was no cause of death in me. But when the Jews spake against it, I was constrained to appeal unto Caesar; not that I had ought to accuse my nation of. For this cause therefore have I called for you, to see you, and to speak with you: because that for the hope of Israel I am bound with this chain." (Acts 28:17-20)

Paul openly acknowledges that he placed himself in the custody of the Romans, but he also makes the point that he was not so much the prisoner of Rome as the prisoner of Christ. It was "for the hope of Israel" that Paul was bound – his commitment to the Gospel and the promise of the kingdom, the hope embodied in the promises to the patriarchs and to David. Paul's determination to serve God rather than man had made him a prisoner. It was the same for Joseph, for Jeremiah, for Daniel and his friends, and for his fellow apostles Peter and John. More importantly, it was for this same hope that his Lord and Saviour had been arrested and crucified.

Paul's detention in Rome lasted for an extended period, during which time he continued to preach boldly to all who came to see him without hindrance:

> "Paul dwelt two whole years in his own hired house, and received all that came in unto him, preaching the kingdom of God, and teaching those things which concern the Lord Jesus Christ, with all confidence, no man forbidding him."
>
> (verses 30,31)

The apostle recognised that he had a divine commission to preach God's word. Just like Jeremiah, regardless of the personal consequences, he had no choice other than to preach. Paul explained to the Corinthians that there was no sense in which he could boast about his preaching; his evangelism was an obligation:

> "For though I preach the gospel, I have nothing to glory of: for necessity is laid upon me; yea, woe is unto me, if I preach not the gospel!" (1 Corinthians 9:16)

"Woe is unto me, if I preach not"! Woe came upon him in Lystra, in Thessalonica and in Jerusalem because he did preach, but remaining silent would have been a greater woe. It simply was not an option.

Paul was born a free man – a Roman citizen, with all the rights and privileges that entailed. Only a small proportion of men at that time were so blessed. Although he was prepared to take advantage of this when appropriate, he did not allow this privilege to override his higher citizenship, his role as a servant, even a prisoner of Christ.

Paul wrote several epistles while a prisoner in Rome. These letters demonstrate that those who are imprisoned for their faith can serve God very effectively, sometimes all the more so because of the circumstances in which they are placed. Paul was an "ambassador in bonds" (Ephesians 6:20) of the Gospel, as were Hanani, Jeremiah and Daniel, and as have been so many faithful brothers and sisters throughout the ages.

The epistle to the Ephesians is one of those believed to have been written by Paul while in Rome. It significant, therefore, as mentioned earlier, that twice in Ephesians Paul refers to himself as the prisoner of Christ. A prisoner has no rights of his own; he must submit to the will of the one who holds him captive. The first reference to Paul as Christ's prisoner is consistent with the statement in 1 Corinthians 9; he links it to his obligation to preach the word:

> "For this cause I Paul, the prisoner of Jesus Christ for you Gentiles, if ye have heard of the dispensation of the grace of God which is given me to you-ward: how that by revelation he made known unto me the mystery; (as I wrote afore in few words, whereby, when ye read, ye may understand my knowledge in the mystery of Christ)."   (Ephesians 3:1-4)

Having reminded them that they had received God's word, Paul goes on in chapter 4 to exhort the Ephesians to unity in the one faith:

> "I therefore, the prisoner of the Lord, beseech you that ye walk worthy of the vocation wherewith ye are called, with all lowliness and meekness, with longsuffering, forbearing one another in love; endeavouring to keep the unity of the Spirit in the bond of peace."   (Ephesians 4:1-3)

Paul the prisoner exhorts us to a life of lowliness, meekness, longsuffering and forbearance. These are all qualities about which a prisoner is qualified to comment. They are the essential prerequisites of life as a prisoner – in the days of the patriarchs, the days of the prophets, the days of the apostles and the times in which we live.

Philippians also was written from Rome, as the reference to the brethren in Caesar's household confirms (Philippians 4:22). In the spirit of Romans 8:28 Paul refers to the positive impact that his confinement has had in Rome, and especially the royal palace:

"I would ye should understand, brethren, that the things which happened unto me have fallen out rather unto the furtherance of the gospel; so that my bonds in Christ are manifest in all the palace, and in all other places."   (Philippians 1:12,13)

The implication is that Paul's example as a prisoner had a profound impact on some members of the royal household. Perhaps it was the influence of some of these converts which accounts for the fact that he was able to enjoy what appears to have been relatively benign home detention in Rome for two years (Acts 28:30), rather than being dealt with more summarily.

There were other benefits for the brotherhood arising from Paul's detention:

"Many of the brethren in the Lord, waxing confident by my bonds, are much more bold to speak the word without fear."
(Philippians 1:14)

Paul's removal from the public arena created both an opportunity and a need for others to fill the gap. That is as it should be, even if not every brother was actuated by a pure motive (verse 15). This did not bother Paul, however, who was pleased that the Gospel was being preached regardless of the circumstances (verses 16-18).

In his letter to the brothers and sisters in Colosse, Paul's passing references to his imprisonment are more muted. He urges them to pray that, in spite of his bonds, his preaching might be effective (Colossians 4:3), before closing with a plea which evokes the exhortation of Hebrews 13:3 that they might "remember my bonds" (Colossians 4:18). It would be naive to imagine that, even for the Apostle Paul, imprisonment would be a time of unalloyed joy, so we should not be perturbed by the sombre overtones here. Light and shade are part of the life of every believer.

We are not told the outcome of the trial that followed Paul's two years of home detention in Rome. Presumably he was acquitted. That may have been in about AD 62. It is widely believed that Paul embarked on further preaching trips following his release from detention in Rome, although it is impossible to say exactly where. Paul had written to the Romans of his interest in visiting Spain (Romans 15:24,28) and since ancient times[2] it has been considered likely that he fulfilled this ambition after his first period of imprisonment in Rome.

"The time of my departure is at hand"

There is some evidence to suggest that the opposition to the Christian community grew more intense in the latter years of Nero's reign (this is discussed in more detail in the next chapter). It would seem that Paul was once again arrested, presumably because he was recognised as a leader of the community, and that on this second occasion the conditions of his imprisonment were not so benign. His discomfort and the anxiety it caused may be detected in comments he made to his beloved "son" Timothy.

In what is thought to be Paul's final letter, 2 Timothy, he refers to his situation as a prisoner. He reminds Timothy that he is in bonds because of the Gospel, but that the Gospel itself is not bound (2 Timothy 2:9). He goes on to warn Timothy, however, that forces were at work which had the potential to thwart the power of God's word (4:3,4). Before he mentions this threat, Paul reminds Timothy of his experiences in Antioch, Iconium and Lystra and the fact that he had been delivered from these persecutions, and that all who follow Christ should expect to

---

2   The apocryphal *Epistle of Clement to the Corinthians*, believed to date from the closing years of the first century, refers in chapter 5 to Paul being released after having been a prisoner, and goes on to speak of the apostle "having taught righteousness unto the whole world and having reached the farthest bounds of the West". If Clement was writing from Rome this could only refer to the Iberian Peninsula.

suffer likewise, and by implication also expect to be delivered (3:10-12).

In chapter 4 Paul speaks as if his death is imminent (verse 6) and expresses a keen desire for Timothy to come to him soon. There is a slight air of despondency about the way he describes his current circumstances in Rome:

"Do thy diligence to come shortly unto me: for Demas hath forsaken me, having loved this present world, and is departed unto Thessalonica; Crescens to Galatia, Titus unto Dalmatia. Only Luke is with me."   (verses 9-11)

This underlines the Lord's reference to the importance of visiting the saints in prison (Matthew 25:34-40) and the exhortation to remember those in bonds (Hebrews 13:3). Even a man as gifted and faithful as Paul, one who was confident that he would be granted immortality on the day of judgement (2 Timothy 4:8), would benefit from the encouragement of visitors while in detention.

Paul goes on to give Timothy instructions about things he should bring with him:

"The cloke that I left at Troas with Carpus, when thou comest, bring with thee, and the books, but especially the parchments."   (verse 13)

What an extraordinary verse! This is more than just a list of objects that might be useful; it embodies an exhortation that all the prisoners of Christ should heed.

Paul asks for his cloke to be brought to Rome. This might seem rather mundane, but an ageing man in detention under abject conditions in a strange city would have great need of a garment which would keep him warm. There is no need for those who are imprisoned to exacerbate their suffering through some vain show of asceticism.

Having mentioned the cloke Paul goes on to ask for "the books, but especially the parchments". It would seem that when Paul speaks of books, he is referring to notes that he may have written, perhaps in his study of God's word. But while these books and the cloke are desired, the things he desires most are the parchments, which would appear to be copies of scripture. Paul's greatest desire as a long-term prisoner was to have ready access to the word of God. There are many legitimate needs that a prisoner might have, but over and above all of them, for Paul this was the greatest need. It was the Gospel which had caused him to be imprisoned but this did not diminish his desire to have access to the word.

In the past many were imprisoned and even executed for daring to possess a copy of God's word. There are places in the world today where it is still illegal to have a Bible. May it be that Paul's example will inspire us to a greater love for God's word.

Paul goes on in 2 Timothy to refer to the fact that he had been abandoned when he was arraigned for trial:

"At my first defence no one came to stand by me, but all deserted me. May it not be charged against them! But the Lord stood by me and strengthened me, so that through me the message might be fully proclaimed and all the Gentiles might hear it. So I was rescued from the lion's mouth."

(2 Timothy 4:16,17, ESV)

When his Master had been arrested all the disciples fled. Although John and Peter later went to the High Priest's home there is no evidence that they were able to render their Lord even moral support during his trial. Paul would no doubt have pondered how his sufferings reflected those of Jesus, and likewise have been aware of the divine strength that God extended to both men in their hour of need.

It is curious to note Paul's reference in verse 17 to being rescued from the lion's mouth. There is, in fact, no evidence that Paul was spared further suffering. In fact it is thought likely that he was executed soon after his final arrest and the penning of this letter to Timothy. Nevertheless he knew that, in Christ, he was more than conqueror and thus he could align himself with Daniel who also was rescued from the lion's mouth.

"Who shall lay any thing to the charge of God's elect? It is God that justifieth. Who is he that condemneth? It is Christ that died, yea rather, that is risen again, who is even at the right hand of God, who also maketh intercession for us. Who shall separate us from the love of Christ? shall tribulation, or distress, or persecution, or famine, or nakedness, or peril, or sword? As it is written, For thy sake we are killed all the day long; we are accounted as sheep for the slaughter. Nay, in all these things we are more than conquerors through him that loved us. For I am persuaded, that neither death, nor life, nor angels, nor principalities, nor powers, nor things present, nor things to come, nor height, nor depth, nor any other creature, shall be able to separate us from the love of God, which is in Christ Jesus our Lord."   (Romans 8:33-39)

Paul concludes his remarks to Timothy about his imprisonment with a confident assertion that reflects the words above that he had written to the Romans:

"The Lord shall deliver me from every evil work, and will preserve me unto his heavenly kingdom: to whom be glory for ever and ever. Amen."   (2 Timothy 4:18)

These words apply to Paul and all the faithful in all ages who suffer persecution and bonds for their faithfulness to the Gospel.

"The love of Christ constrains me"

W HEN Joseph was imprisoned by Potiphar in Egypt his fellow inmates were referred to as "prisoners" (Genesis 39:20,22), using the Hebrew *ah-seer*. That same word is used sometimes in the poetical books to refer to those who have died and who are now held securely in the grave (e.g., Job 3:18; Psalm 107:10). It is also used to refer to those who are subject to bondage under the law of sin of death:

> "Let the sighing of the prisoner come before thee; according to the greatness of thy power preserve thou those that are appointed to die." (Psalm 79:11)

> "To hear the groaning of the prisoner; to loose those that are appointed to death." (102:20)

All the sons of Adam are prisoners whether they realise it or not. They all are appointed to die. Without Christ, they all are in bondage to sin and death. But like Joseph, Jeremiah, Daniel, Daniel's friends and Peter, all these prisoners can be delivered if they put their faith in God. Like Paul, all these prisoners can find the strength to endure the constraints of imprisonment if they put their faith in God and if they seek to align themselves to the example of their Lord Jesus Christ.

> "In writing about drug abuse, one addict noted it was when he determined to understand the 'Bible teaching regarding the crucifixion' that his life was changed. The outpouring of divine love evident in the way of redemption evoked a response of love from his own heart … The power of the cross to work

moral and spiritual change in our life has been to supersede legalistic explanations and technical definitions."[1]

A servant of Christ

It was so for Paul who rejoiced "in imprisonments" (2 Corinthians 6:5), not because he was a masochist but because he was a committed follower of his Lord. He did not rejoice in suffering out of a sense of vainglorious self-promotion – 'Look at me and see what a stalwart disciple of the Lord I am, willing to endure terrible persecution!' Self-promotion was the furthest thing from Paul's mind. His service was all about his crucified and risen Lord, not about Paul:

> "For we preach not ourselves, but Christ Jesus the Lord; and ourselves your servants for Jesus' sake. For God, who commanded the light to shine out of darkness, hath shined in our hearts, to give the light of the knowledge of the glory of God in the face of Jesus Christ. But we have this treasure in earthen vessels, that the excellency of the power may be of God, and not of us." (4:5-7)

We are all members of the body of Christ – this was a major theme of the first letter to the Corinthians and Paul returns to it in this second letter. Our work as the servants of the Lord is the work of the Lord. When we recognise our true position, described in verse 5 as servants, we shall appreciate that we cannot shrug off this responsibility and expect our Master to approve of our actions.

Do we regard ourselves as inadequate to the challenge? Do we think that we are not articulate enough, not educated enough, not outgoing enough to preach? If so, so much the better! This is not about self-promotion. Notice that in this passage Paul uses the plural pronoun "we" (indeed throughout this chapter from verse 1). "We", he says, not 'ye'. We have this treasure in earthen vessels. It is true that Paul was a skilled orator, he was well educated, he was outgoing, but he still recognised that he

---

1   Don Styles, *Essays to Believers*, Christadelphian Tidings Publications (2008), page 201.

was a frail earthen vessel. As one of our hymns puts it, "How frail, at best, is dying man!" Remember the example of Moses. He believed that he was inadequate for the task assigned to him by God, but God made it clear that his own prowess was of no relevance. It matters not how inadequate we might perceive ourselves to be – in fact in some respects the more inadequate the better – because the power of the Gospel is derived not from us but from God.

Like the reference to light shining out of darkness (verse 6), the term "earthen vessels" (verse 7) takes our mind back to Genesis. Man was created from the dust of the ground. Only when man and woman had been created was the whole creation pronounced "very good". The corrupting, dishonest reasoning of the serpent marred that creation, but it could not frustrate the grace of God. God had made man from the dust with the object of filling the earth with His glory. Now Paul reminds us that God is still working with the sons of Adam to bring many sons to glory. The treasure is still in vessels of earth, but God's power can work its transforming miracle through Christ.

Paul then goes on in one of his most eloquent passages to describe the emotional turmoil he experienced on a daily basis:

"We are troubled on every side, yet not distressed; we are perplexed, but not in despair; persecuted, but not forsaken; cast down, but not destroyed."   (verses 8,9)

This is not just vain triumphalism. Paul is describing real turmoil as he sets out the daily stresses he endures, especially in relation to the "care of all the ecclesias". As was the case with Moses, Paul's leadership role was stressful. He was pushed to the limit, and it was only his faith in God and his reliance on God's strength that helped him through.

While we might never be called upon to face the extreme trials that Paul describes in 2 Corinthians, we can take comfort from his example. When the difficulties of our daily round threaten to swamp us, let us remember this exhortation and remember that we shall not be overwhelmed. If Paul was not conquered, our minor inconveniences should never bring us down.

Paul saw the challenges and trials he faced in the context of the sacrifice of our Lord:

> "Always bearing about in the body the dying of the Lord Jesus, that the life also of Jesus might be made manifest in our body. For we which live are alway delivered unto death for Jesus' sake, that the life also of Jesus might be made manifest in our mortal flesh."   (2 Corinthians 4:10,11)

Paul, inspired and driven by the mercy of God, now draws even closer to the sacrifice of Christ. He links his own ministry with the suffering of the Lord on the cross. What are we to make of this? What point is being made for the benefit of the Corinthians and for us?

At one level Paul is drawing our attention to the fact that, as members of the body of Christ, the life we now live is the life of Christ. We crucified the old man at our baptism and we now live the life of the resurrected Christ. This is a first principle concept that we learn from places such as Romans 6 and Galatians 2. But Paul's point in this passage is more personal and profound: there is a deeper layer of meaning in these verses.

Paul links his trials with the trials and agonies of the Master. This might seem a little presumptuous, yet it is a recurring theme in his writings. In the account of his conversion on the Damascus Road we find the first reference to this theme. When the Lord told Ananias to go to meet Saul and cure his blindness, Ananias was shocked. The Lord reassured him that the persecuting Saul was a changed man and that he had a mission to perform as a servant of Christ:

> "The Lord said unto [Ananias], Arise, and go into the street which is called Straight, and inquire in the house of Judas for one called Saul, of Tarsus: for, behold, he prayeth, and hath seen in a vision a man named Ananias coming in, and putting his hand on him, that he might receive his sight. Then Ananias answered, Lord, I have heard by many of this man, how much evil he hath done to thy saints at Jerusalem: and here he hath authority from the chief priests to bind all that call on thy name. But the Lord said unto him, Go thy way: for

he is a chosen vessel unto me, to bear my name before the Gentiles, and kings, and the children of Israel: for I will shew him how great things *he must suffer for my name's sake*."

(Acts 9:11-16)

The fellowship of his sufferings

At the very beginning of his ministry Paul was told that he must suffer many things for the Gospel. We have already read of these sufferings. In Philippians Paul specifically links his sufferings with the crucifixion and testifies that nothing is more important than becoming associated in a direct and real way with the sufferings of Christ:

"But what things were gain to me, those I counted loss for Christ. Yea doubtless, and I count all things but loss for the excellency of the knowledge of Christ Jesus my Lord: for whom I have suffered the loss of all things, and do count them but dung, that I may win Christ, and be found in him, not having mine own righteousness, which is of the law, but that which is through the faith of Christ, the righteousness which is of God by faith: that I may know him, and the power of his resurrection, and the fellowship of his sufferings, being made conformable unto his death; if by any means I might attain unto the resurrection of the dead."   (Philippians 3:7-11)

His point is made even more strikingly in Colossians:

"Who now rejoice in my sufferings for you, and fill up that which is behind of the afflictions of Christ in my flesh for his body's sake, which is the ecclesia."   (Colossians 1:24)

This is a confronting verse. We can understand how Paul could accept his sufferings as the price of having preached the Gospel to those in darkness, but the second half of this verse poses a real challenge to our minds.

The KJV rendering, "fill up that which is behind of the afflictions of Christ in my flesh" may mask the enormity of what Paul says. The RSV reads, "in my flesh I complete what is lacking in Christ's afflictions". The NIV renders it as, "I fill up in my flesh what is still lacking in regard to Christ's afflictions". The ESV,

Weymouth, Young's Literal Translation and many others confirm that Paul is speaking of how his sufferings fill up that which is lacking in the sacrifice of Christ.

Paul was in no doubt about the all-sufficiency and efficacy of Christ's death. Christ's atoning work on the cross was final: nothing else was needed. That message is reiterated throughout the Acts and the epistles. So in what sense can Paul suggest that he needed to suffer to fill up what was lacking in this work?

Paul's point in 2 Corinthians 4, Philippians 3 and Colossians 1 would seem to be this. He rejoiced in his afflictions because it was appropriate that, as the representative of Christ (his ambassador, 2 Corinthians 5:20), he should suffer to the same extent that his Master would suffer if he were acting in his own person rather than through his agent Paul. Paul's willingness to suffer was not vain asceticism. He was not seeking agony as some form of bizarre personal act of will-worship. No, he endured these agonies for the sake of the ecclesia. As we saw in 2 Corinthians, Paul was motivated by his appreciation of the mercy of God and he was determined to bring that hope to others.

Paul's situation was somewhat rare, so his example in this rather extreme matter might seem remote to us. But Peter takes this principle to a personal level, one to which we might relate more readily:

> "Forasmuch then as Christ hath suffered for us in the flesh, arm yourselves likewise with the same mind: for he that hath suffered in the flesh hath ceased from sin; that he no longer should live the rest of his time in the flesh to the lusts of men, but to the will of God."   (1 Peter 4:1,2)

We have crucified the old man and now live as members of the body of Christ. We no longer serve the flesh. On the contrary, we are servants of God and therefore, like Paul, the prisoners of Christ.

The mercy of God was an all-encompassing and motivating force in the life of Paul: it must be so also for us. "For the love of Christ constraineth us" (2 Corinthians 5:14) (Weymouth: "the love of Christ overmasters us"). The love of God as seen in

Christ Jesus must motivate us to a life of faithful service even, when necessary, in the face of persecution, imprisonment or, in extreme circumstances, death.

Imprisonment and death were a real threat to our brothers and sisters in the days of the apostles. At times they were left largely unmolested but at other times they were very actively persecuted. At the end of the first century, in the Lord's letter to Smyrna, the members of the ecclesia were both warned and encouraged about an impending threat to their life and liberty:

"Fear none of those things which thou shalt suffer: behold, the devil shall cast some of you into prison, that ye may be tried; and ye shall have tribulation ten days: be thou faithful unto death, and I will give thee a crown of life."

(Revelation 2:10)

The believers in Smyrna are warned to expect a period of persecution. Some were to be cast into prison. The language used makes it clear that, at least in certain cases, some also would suffer the death penalty. Brother John Thomas and others have interpreted this as a reference to the persecution of Christians which occurred during the reign of the Roman emperor Trajan, who ascended the imperial throne in AD 98 and reigned till AD 117.

Pliny to Trajan

A remarkable ancient document gives us insight into this period of persecution. One of Trajan's provincial governors was a man named Pliny who presided over the Roman province of Bithynia, which is relatively close to Smyrna. In about AD 112 Pliny wrote to the emperor seeking guidance as to how he should deal with Christians brought to him for punishment. The letter is interesting not just for the way in which it confirms the words of Revelation 2:10, but for the insights it provides into the life of believers at the beginning of the second century and how they responded more or less positively to the persecution of the state:

"I never had the fortune to be present at any examination of Christians, before I came into this province. I am therefore at a loss to determine what is the usual object either of inquiry or of punishment, and to what length either of them is to be carried. It has also been a question with me very problematical, whether any distinction should be made between the young and the old, the tender and the robust, whether any room should be given for repentance, or the guilt of Christianity once incurred is not to be expiated by the most unequivocal retraction; whether the name itself, abstracted from any flagitiousness of conduct, or the crimes connected with the name, be the object of punishment. In the meantime, this has been my method with respect to those who were brought before me as Christians.

"I asked them whether they were Christians: if they pleaded guilty, I interrogated them twice afresh, with a menace of capital punishment. In case of obstinate perseverance, I ordered them to be executed. For of this I had no doubt, whatever was the nature of their religion, that a sullen and obstinate inflexibility called for the vengeance of the magistrate. Some were infected with the same madness whom, on account of their privilege of citizenship, I reserved to be sent to Rome, to be referred to your tribunal.

"In the course of this business, informations pouring in, as is usual when they are encouraged, more cases occurred. An anonymous libel was exhibited, with a catalogue of names of persons, who yet declared that they were not Christians then, nor ever had been; and they repeated after me an invocation of the gods and of your image, which, for this purpose, I had ordered to be brought with the images of the deities: they performed sacred rites with wine and frankincense, and execrated Christ – none of which things I am told a real Christian can ever be compelled to do. On this account I dismissed them. Others named by an informer, first affirmed, and then denied the charge of Christianity; declaring that they had been Christians, but had ceased to be so some three years ago, others still longer, some even twenty years ago. All of them worshipped your image, and the statues of the gods, and also execrated Christ.

"And this was the account which they gave of the nature of the religion they once had professed, whether it deserves the name of crime or error; namely, that they were accustomed on a stated day to meet before daylight, and to repeat among themselves a hymn to Christ as to a god, and to bind themselves by an oath, with an obligation of not committing any wickedness; but on the contrary, of abstaining from thefts, robberies, and adulteries; also of not violating their promise, or denying a pledge; after which it was their custom to separate, and to meet again at a promiscuous harmless meal, from which last practice they however desisted, after the publication of my edict, in which, agreeably to your orders, I forbade any societies of that sort. On which account, I judged it the more necessary to inquire by torture from two females, who were said to be deaconesses, what is the real truth. But nothing could I collect, except a depraved and excessive superstition. Deferring therefore any further investigation, I determined to consult you. For the number of culprits is so great as to call for serious consultation. Many persons are informed against, of every age and of both sexes; and more still will be in the same situation. The contagion of the superstition hath spread not only through cities, but even villages and the country. Not that I think it impossible to check and correct it. The success of my endeavours hitherto forbids such desponding thoughts: for the temples once almost desolate, begin to be frequented, and the sacred solemnities, which had long been intermitted, are now attended afresh; and the sacrificial victims are now sold everywhere, which once could scarcely find a purchaser. Whence I conclude that many might be reclaimed, were the hope of impunity, on repentance, absolutely confirmed."[2]

---

2   Pliny (the Younger) to Trajan. *Pliny Epp. X (ad Traj.), xcvi.* As quoted in J. Thomas, *Eureka*, volume 1, pages 254,255.

The love of God

For most of us, especially those who live in liberal, Western societies, severe persecution such as that experienced under Trajan is unlikely; even imprisonment is likely only when the country in which we reside as a stranger and a pilgrim is seriously threatened by war, and often not even then. But there are daily opportunities to reflect the love extended by God to us. The love of God in Christ should constrain us so to act.

> "Therefore if any man be in Christ, he is a new creature: old things are passed away; behold, all things are become new. And all things are of God, who hath reconciled us to himself by Jesus Christ, and hath given to us the ministry of reconciliation; to wit, that God was in Christ, reconciling the world unto himself, not imputing their trespasses unto them; and hath committed unto us the word of reconciliation. Now then we are ambassadors for Christ, as though God did beseech you by us: we pray you in Christ's stead, be ye reconciled to God."   (2 Corinthians 5:17-20)

Might we all feel the power of John's words and find in them a stimulus to ongoing zeal in the service of our Master, our brethren and those in darkness at all times whether we are enjoying liberty or suffering in bonds for the sake of our Lord:

> "Hereby perceive we the love of God, because he laid down his life for us: and we ought to lay down our lives for the brethren."   (1 John 3:16)

8 |

Epilogue

HEBREWS 11 and its catalogue of the faithful is a familiar record but it is always inspiring. One of the people we have considered is mentioned explicitly in the chapter: Joseph is referred to in verse 22. Jeremiah and Daniel are there implicitly in verse 32 when the prophets are mentioned. The example of these faithful men, and of the others listed in Hebrews 11, encourages us to endure to the end. And they have inspired our brethren in other ages who have faced trials much more severe than any we have encountered. The author sums up his remarks in verses 32 to 38. There are in these verses unmistakable allusions to Daniel, Joseph, Jeremiah, Daniel's friends and Peter:

"And what shall I more say? for the time would fail me to tell of Gedeon, and of Barak, and of Samson, and of Jephthae; of David also, and Samuel, and of the prophets: who through faith subdued kingdoms, wrought righteousness, obtained promises, stopped the mouths of lions, quenched the violence of fire, escaped the edge of the sword, out of weakness were made strong, waxed valiant in fight, turned to flight the armies of the aliens. Women received their dead raised to life again: and others were tortured, not accepting deliverance; that they might obtain a better resurrection: and others had trial of cruel mockings and scourgings, yea, moreover of bonds and imprisonment: they were stoned, they were sawn asunder, were tempted, were slain with the sword: they wandered about in sheepskins and goatskins; being destitute, afflicted, tormented; (of whom the world was not worthy:) they wandered in deserts, and in mountains, and in dens and caves of the earth."   (Hebrews 11:32-38)

In verse 38 we read that the world was not worthy of these men. In every sense the world was not worthy. They endured to the end against considerable opposition and they inspire us to do likewise. They will, if we recognise and really believe the words with which the chapter concludes:

"These all, having obtained a good report through faith, received not the promise: God having provided some better thing for us, that they without us should not be made perfect."   (Hebrews 11:39,40)

Scripture index